St. Mark's Church in the Bowery

Memorial of St. Mark's Church in the Bowery

Containing an account of the services held to commemorate the one-hundredth anniversary of the dedication of the church

St. Mark's Church in the Bowery

Memorial of St. Mark's Church in the Bowery
Containing an account of the services held to commemorate the one-hundredth anniversary of the dedication of the church

ISBN/EAN: 9783337111144

Printed in Europe, USA, Canada, Australia, Japan

Cover: Foto ©ninafisch / pixelio.de

More available books at **www.hansebooks.com**

CONTENTS.

	PAGE.
The Centennial Services:	
Account of Services, Programmes, etc.	5
Sermon of Bishop Potter	11
Address of Dr. Huntington	25
" " " Coe	28
" " Dean Van Amringe	34
" " Dr. Richey	37
" " " Dix	43
Brief biographies of the rectors:	
John Callahan	66
William Harris	70
William Creighton	78
Henry Anthon	84
Alex. H. Vinton	94
Joseph H. Rylance	101
An historical sketch of the church	106
APPENDIX:	
Wardens and vestrymen, 1799–1899	161
Treasurers of the vestry	164
Clerks of the vestry	"
Pewholders at different periods	166
Assistant-ministers in charge at the chapel	172
Organists and organs	173
Sextons	"
Memorial Tablets	174
" Windows	182
Certificate of first incorporation	185
Opinion of counsel	186
Quit-claim deed given to Trinity Church	"
Deed for a pew in St. Mark's Church	188
Copies of letters:	
(*a*) John Henry Hobart	189
(*b*) Philander Chase	"
(*c*) Cave Jones	190
(*d*) Theodore Dehon	191
Annual Memorial Service, All Saints' Day	193

LIST OF ILLUSTRATIONS.

	PAGE
St. Mark's, on May 9th, 1899 (exterior)............Frontispiece.	
" " " " " " (interior).......................	43
" " in 1799..	112
" " in 1899 (exterior).................................	150
" " " " (interior)..............................	156
" " Chapel and Parish House........................	154

Portraits of the Rectors:

    Mr. Callahan, from a miniature on ivory in the possession of Henry Dudley, Esq., of New York.............. 66

    Dr. Harris, from an oil painting in the possession of Columbia University.................................... 70

    " Creighton, from a photograph in the possession of the Rev. J. Selden Spencer, Tarrytown, N. Y.......... 78

    " Anthon, from an oil painting in the possession of St. Mark's Church..................................... 84

    " Vinton, from a photograph by Notman, of Boston, Mass... 94

    " Rylance, from a photograph by Fredericks, New York. 101

Governor Stuyvesant's Tomb........................ 179

The Centennial Services.

An account of the services held in St. Mark's Church, on Sunday, May 7, 1899, and Tuesday, May 9, 1899, to commemorate the one-hundredth anniversary of the dedication of the church, on May 9, 1799, with the sermon preached by the Rt. Rev. the Bishop of the diocese on Sunday morning, the addresses made by the Rev. Drs. Huntington, Coe and Richey, and Dean Van Amringe, on Sunday evening, and the historical address delivered by the Rev. Dr. Dix on Tuesday at noon.

As the one-hundredth anniversary of the consecration of St. Mark's Church approached, the vestry resolved to celebrate the interesting event by a series of services, differing in character and affording opportunity for the participation of the present representatives of the various churches and other institutions in the city of New York, which have had an historical connection with St. Mark's during the past century.

The anniversary day, May 9th, fell on a Tuesday, and it was therefore decided to begin the celebration on the preceding Sunday and to request the Bishop of the diocese to preach on

Sunday, and the rector of Trinity to deliver an historical address on Tuesday.

The institutions which it was desired to have represented, and the reasons therefor, are as follows:

Trinity, as the "mother of churches" in New York, to whom St. Mark's largely owes its existence; St. George's, St. Paul's, Christ Church and the French Church du St. Esprit, as being the only other ones organized before St. Mark's; the Collegiate Dutch Church, as St. Mark's stands partly on the site of Gov. Peter Stuyvesant's chapel; the General Theological Seminary, as the land which it occupies was given by a member of St. Mark's—Clement C. Moore— and another member—Peter Gerard Stuyvesant —endowed the St. Mark's Church in the Bowery Professorship of Ecclesiastical History; Columbia University, the second rector of St. Mark's, the Rev. Dr. Harris, having been at the same time president of Columbia College; the Anthon Memorial Church, because it was founded by St. Mark's Church. It also seemed fitting to invite the rectors of the neighboring parishes and former assistant-ministers of St. Mark's. This general plan was carried into effect—a few only of those invited being unable to accept—in the manner detailed in the copy of the order of exercises which follows:

SUNDAY, MAY 7TH, AT 11 A.M.
  Conducted by the Rev. C. H. Babcock, D.D., the minister in charge, the Ven. Archdeacon C. C. Tiffany, D.D., the Very Rev. Dean E. A. Hoffman, D.C.L., and the Rev. Walter Dela-

field, D.D., with Sermon by the Rt. Rev. the Bishop of the Diocese.

SUNDAY, MAY 7TH, AT 8 P.M.
Conducted by the minister in charge and the Rev. Messrs. A. C. Kimber, D.D., T. R. Harris, D.D., and W. M. Geer, with addresses by the Rev. Drs. Huntington, Coe and Richey, and Dean Van Amringe, of Columbia University.

TUESDAY, MAY 9TH, AT 12 M.
Conducted by the minister in charge, the Ven. Archdeacon C. C. Tiffany, D.D., and the Rev. Messrs. Percy S. Grant and Wm. R. Harris,* with an historical address by the Rector of Trinity Parish.

CHOIR.

Mrs. Caroline Mihr-Hardy, Soprano.
Miss Miriam C. Griswold, Alto.
Mr. Bayard Hawthorne, Tenor.
Mr. John C. Dempsey, Basso.

Mr. Willis Howard Alling, Organist.
Mr. Wm. Edward Mulligan (invited), Organist.
AND A PICKED CHORUS OF TWENTY VOICES.

Choirmaster,
Mr. John C. Dempsey.

SUNDAY MORNING, MAY 7TH.

ORGAN PRELUDE......................................*C. M. Widor*
PROCESSIONAL, Hymn No. 520........................*Messiter*
VENITE..*Plain Chant*
TE DEUM LAUDAMUS..............................*Dudley Buck*
JUBILATE DEO......................................*Miles B. Foster*
INTROIT, Hymn No. 194............................*H. W. Parker*
KYRIE ELEISON...*Gounod*
HYMN No. 391..*Rossini*
SERMON, by the Rt. Rev. Henry C. Potter, D.D., LL.D., D.C.L.
OFFERTORY ANTHEM, from "Stabat Mater."..............*Rossini*
SANCTUS ....*Dykes*
COMMUNION, Hymn No. 225..............................*Hodges*
GLORIA IN EXCELSIS..................................*Old Chant*
RECESSIONAL, Hymn No. 521.........................*Bainbridge*
POSTLUDE, March Religeuse.................... *Alex. Guilmant*

*A grandson of the second rector of St. Mark's.

SUNDAY EVENING.

ORGAN PRELUDE, Priere Op. 16...................*Alex. Guilmant*
PROCESSIONAL, Hymn No. 512..........................*Beethoven*
PSALTER, Psalm No. 148.............................*Plain Chant*
MAGNIFICAT, in B flat............................*H. W. Parker*
HYMN No. 485...*Williams*
ADDRESS, Rev. Wm. R. Huntington, D.D., Rector of Grace Church.
    Rev. Edward B. Coe, D.D., Senior Minister of the Collegiate Dutch Church.
    Rev. Jacob S. Shipman, D.C.L., Rector of Christ Church.
    Prof. J. H. Van Amringe, LL.D., Dean of Columbia University.
    Rev. Thomas Richey, D.D., St. Mark's Professor of Ecclesiastical History in the General Theological Seminary.
    Rev. Wm. S. Rainsford D.D., Rector of St. George's Church.
OFFERTORY ANTHEM, " The Radiant Morn Hath Passed Away "
                                                                      Woodward
HYMN No. 490..*Haydn*
RECESSIONAL, Hymn No. 679.............................*Stainer*
POSTLUDE, Coronation March...........................*Svendsen*

TUESDAY, NOON, MAY 9TH.

ORGAN PRELUDE, Adagio in F Minor....................*G. Merkel*
PROCESSIONAL HYMN,

Lift the strain of high thanksgiving!
  Tread with songs the hallowed way!
Praise our fathers' God for mercies
  New to us, their sons, to-day:
Here they built for Him a dwelling,
  Served Him here in ages past,
Fixed it for His sure possession,
  Holy ground while time shall last.

Entering, then, Thy gates with praises,
  Lord, be ours Thine Israel's prayer!
" Rise into Thy place of resting,
  Show Thy promised presence there!"

Let the gracious words be spoken
  Here as once on Sion's height,
"This shall be My rest forever,
  This My dwelling of delight."

Praise to Thee, almighty Father,
  Praise to Thee, eternal Son,
Praise to Thee, all-quickening Spirit,
  Ever blessed, three in one.

Threefold Power and Grace and Wisdom
  Moulding out of sinful clay
Living stones for that true temple
  Which shall never know decay.

SENTENCES.
LORD'S PRAYER.
VERSICLES.
PSALTER, Psalms Nos. 48 and 84.....................*Plain Chant*
LESSON, Third Chapter of the Epistle to the Ephesians.
JUBILATE DEO, in B flat............................*H. R. Shelley*
THE APOSTLES' CREED.

COLLECT FOR THE DAY.

O Lord, from whom all good things do come; Grant to us, Thy humble servants, that by Thy holy inspiration we may think the things that are good, and by Thy merciful guiding may perform the same; through our Lord Jesus Christ. *Amen.*

A PRAYER FOR OUR COUNTRY.

Almighty God, who in the former time didst lead our fathers forth into a wealthy place; Give Thy grace, we humbly beseech Thee, to us their children, that we may always approve ourselves a people mindful of Thy favour, and glad to do Thy will. Bless our land with honourable industry, sound learning and pure manners. Defend our liberties, preserve our unity. Save us from violence, discord and confusion, from pride and arrogancy, and from every evil way. Fashion into one happy people the multitude brought hither out of many kindreds and tongues. Endue with the spirit of wisdom those whom we entrust in Thy Name with the authority of governance, to the end that there may be peace at home, and that we keep a place among the nations of the earth. In the time of prosperity, fill our hearts with thankfulness; and in the day of trouble, suffer not our trust in Thee to fail; all which we ask for Jesus Christ's sake. *Amen.*

A PRAYER FOR OUR CHURCH.

Almighty God, who hast in all ages showed forth Thy power and mercy in the preservation of Thy Church and in the protection of all those who do unto Thee true and laudable service, we give Thee thanks for Thy Blessing upon this Church and Parish from the day of its foundation in Thy faith and fear until this hour. We praise Thy name as for all Thy mercies, so especially for the grace which has been ministered and the gospel which has been proclaimed within these walls; for the men of eminence and piety whom Thou hast given as the guides and pastors of this Thy flock, and for the light and truth which Thou hast sent forth from this place to guide the feet of Thy people into the way of peace. O God, we have heard with our ears and our fathers have declared unto us the noble works that Thou didst in their days and in the old time before them. Arise, help us and deliver us for Thine honour. Give us grace that we may follow our fathers as they followed Christ. Make us mindful of the time when we shall be called to give account of our stewardship in Thy Kingdom, and grant us help and strength from on high, that we may be found watching in the day of Thy visitation, steadfast in the faith, fulfilling Thy will, looking for and hastening unto the coming of the day of God. All which we ask in the name and for the sake of Thy Son, our Saviour Jesus Christ. *Amen.*

ANTHEM, from "The Creation"..........................*Haydn*

    The heavens are telling the glory of God,
    The wonder of His works displays the firmament.
    The day that is coming speaks it to-day;
    The night that is gone to following night.
    In all the lands resounds the word,
    Never unperceived, ever understood.

AN HISTORICAL ADDRESS, by the Rev. Morgan Dix, D.D., D.C.L.

TE DEUM, in E flat...............................*Dudley Buck*

COLLECT.

O God, Holy Ghost, Sanctifier of the faithful, visit, we pray Thee, this congregation with Thy love and favour; enlighten their minds more and more with the light of the everlasting Gospel; graft in their hearts a love of the truth; increase in them true religion; nourish them with all goodness; and of Thy great

mercy keep them in the same, O blessed Spirit, Whom, with the Father and the Son together, we worship and glorify as one God, world without end. *Amen.*
BENEDICTION.
RECESSIONAL, Hymn No. 485............................*Williams*
POSTLUDE, Toccata and Fugue in D Minor............*J. S. Bach*

Both Sunday and Tuesday were pleasant days and large congregations were present at all the services. Among them were members of many of the families who worshipped in old St. Mark's in bygone years.

The church was simply but beautifully decorated with living plants placed in the windows and palms in the chancel, and white lilies on the communion table.

On the Anniversary Day, in addition to the flowers, the national colors were used with pleasing effect. Outside, the porch was covered with them, and within they were draped around the galleries and organ loft.

Sermon on Sunday Morning, May 7th, by the Right Rev. the Bishop of New York.

And thine age shall be clear as the noon-day; thou shalt shine forth, thou shalt be as the morning.—JOB xi. 17.

This is the prophecy of Zophar the Naamathite concerning his friend Job. There had been sorrow and disaster in Job's life—a great deal of them; and his friends, with that familiar stupidity which is fond of saying, "I told you so," had set themselves to explaining it. They had not been eminently successful; and their criticisms had shown neither sympathetic insight nor the smallest trace of a sweet reasonableness. In these respects, indeed, the lugubrious utterances of Zophar had been as obtuse and as infelicitous as the rest of them.

Now and then, however, they had stumbled upon a large truth, and the verse which I have repeated is one of them. "Whatever your past," is its meaning, "under God, the future still remains to you." The earlier years may have had their sorrows and shadows; but with time, to him who lifts his life to the level of high ideals, there shall come the day of light and triumph. The truth shall "shine forth"; and he who trusts and lives it shall "be as the morning."

The words are even more true of institutions than of men. Not always here, in individual history, is one whose aims have been high, whose walk has been blameless, whose service has been neither sordid nor ignoble, either vindicated or understood. We look confidently, in the case of such, to their ultimate vindication and recognition—but not always on this stage, nor in their own day. Later generations may, indeed, sometimes do them justice, but even this is not invariably the case.

But with an institution it is different. History has shown to us for our encouragement how often the organized life of a community, a nation, a society, may rise out of a less glorious past to a more potent and illustrious future; and of no other institution is this more true than of that most venerable and sacred of all institutions, both human and divine, the Church of Jesus Christ. It has had its dark days as well as its bright days; ages of apathy and corruption as well as those of purity and zeal; but, more than once, from times of weakness and failure, it has gone on to victories of glorious and heroic mould.

You will understand why my thoughts run in such a current as this when I remind you of the beginnings to which this anniversary takes us back, and the conditions and characteristics which distinguished them. If St. Mark's Church has reached the age of one hundred years, that means that it began its corporate existence in the year 1799. It does not belong to me to present to you the historical review of the century that has elapsed since then—which is a task to be performed, on Tuesday next, by another, far more competent. My office, as I interpret it, is rather to turn your faces from the past to the present and the future—to recognize the significance of the one, and to discern, if we may, the obligations which belong to the other.

But we cannot discharge such a duty without at least recognizing what those original conditions were, out of which our present has grown; nor without tracing, however hastily, the sequence of those influences that have created the situation which at present exists.

A living Church historian has described the period in our American Church history between 1789 and 1811 as "a period of suspended animation and feeble growth,"* and it must be owned that such a designation of it is substantially accurate. It would take me too far afield to show this from its history as a whole, nor indeed is such an excursion at all necessary, for its history in this diocese is an abundant demonstration of the fact. The Bishop of New York from 1787 to 1815 was Samuel Provoost. As his name implies, he was of Huguenot descent; and his attachment to his native land and to its institutions was rather that of a patriot than an ecclesiastic. Indeed, his selection for his office was probably determined by considerations of

* "American Church History," Tiffany, p. 385.

the former quite as much as the latter character. At any rate, the most amiable estimate of his character could hardly have described him as an ardent Churchman, and it is certain that he had no very sanguine expectations as to the growth of the Church, or its mission to his age and countrymen. He is said, indeed, to have expressed the opinion that the Church in the United States would die out with the old colonial families; and with such views it was not to be expected that he should do much to promote its growth or advancement. He was "an accomplished scholar and a good botanist," and neither as an ecclesiastical statesman nor a theologian did he discover any purposes that were either resolute or aggressive. Nor, if he had, is it probable that he would have won any considerable following. The Episcopal Church had been the Church of the Royalists; it was still largely the Church of the aristocrats. Its worship was condemned as cold and formal—and I am afraid that very often it was; and its preaching was tame and decorous, but not greatly marked either by spiritual insight or a lofty enthusiasm.

Under such circumstances not much was to be expected in the City of New York in the way of Church growth, and as a matter of fact very little was accomplished. And yet these were the circumstances under which St. Mark's Church came into existence. You will be told hereafter whose was the initiative, and what were the co-operating forces. But, though it is not mine to speak of these, we may wisely recognize how unlike to the present situation was that which existed then. New York has never been a homogeneous city, of one race, sprung from one stock, with one ecclesiastical communion to represent to it the idea of religion, and it was not then. There were the Dutch foundations, with their Dutch Reformed Churches, the English superimposition with its Anglo-American Communion, and the Lutheran and Huguenot Congregations, with, here and there, communities which stood for New England Congregationalism; but beyond this there was little or nothing to answer to that wide diversity of race, of creed, of social beliefs and aspirations which makes the New York of our time the vast and unassimilated mass of most heterogeneous and often hostile elements that it is to-day.

And so this Church, begun in 1799, took up the line of decorous conservatism in worship and teaching which was in fact expected of it. At the time of its organization it stood amid the homes of those whose family names are still familiar to some of us, and whose social standing and personal character were among the foremost. Whoever they were, whether of English, Dutch, or any other descent, they saw in the institutions of religion the one enduring foundation of a State, and in the teachings of Jesus Christ the highest hope, whether of nations or of men. Infidelity of both the critical and the vulgar type was rife in the land, and had, in Jefferson and in Thomas Paine, characteristic and influential representatives. But their feet, who organized the parish, had not strayed from the old paths, and were not moved from the one Rock. That they might worship as their fathers had worshipped; that their children might be taught as they had been taught; that the community in which they lived might continue to be made up of respectable and God-fearing people; whatever might be the apostasies of wayward and ill-regulated minds, this, I suppose, was in substance their hope and their expectation. They had indeed launched a young Republic. They had, verily, broken with some of the most venerable and sacred traditions of their forefathers; but they believed firmly that God had shown them the way in their national progress, and that He would enable them to hold fast to the faith and the worship of their past.

If one can transport himself out of our New York of to-day, and go back in spirit to that time when St. Mark's was born, he must needs become sensible, I think, of an element in it all of singular pathos. How utterly impossible would it have been, men and brethren, for your predecessors who first sat in these pews to conceive of the present situation! Then, indeed, their civic order was new and untried, and there were the restlessness, the sharp differences of opinion and of association which were inseparable from such a situation. But, on the other hand, the religious mind of the Christian world was agitated by no grave questions, and held rather to its ancient spiritual inheritance in a mood of decorous quiescence. And more than this, though the French Revolution of 1789 was not long past, the social order of Christendom rested largely in almost equally ancient and inflexible moulds.

But to you and me, whether we choose to see it or no, there has come, at any rate in the domain of religion, and with reference to all those august and sacred interests for which this Church is here, a new day with largely new demands. The era of submission, whether blindly or conventionally—whether because men do not know, or because they do not think—to mere authority is ended. It is not that in things spiritual there is no longer place for authority—if that were so, then surely the fabric of our hopes would ere long be crumbling about our ears—it is that the *basis* of authority is not, and cannot be, any longer in the mere claim, whether in things temporal or things spiritual—but supremely in this latter realm—of those who assert it. After ages of traditional reverence, whether for a man or for a book, the world has come back to that one final ground of authority which Jesus Christ proclaimed when He said :

"If I do not the works of my Father, believe me not. But if I do, though ye believe not me, believe the works; that ye may know and believe that the Father is in me and I in him."*

*St. John x. 37, 38.

My brethren of this ancient and honored parish, I congratulate you with all my heart upon the record of that past which lies behind you to-day. I rejoice with you in the long bede-roll of saints and servants of God, who, whether in the ministry or out of it, have wrought here and worshipped here. I rejoice with you that this Church stands unmoved, and substantially unchanged, upon its ancient and stable spiritual foundations; that the prayers of our fathers are still uplifted here; and that His Word, written and preached, has been so long heard and His Holy Sacraments continuously administered within these sacred walls.

But what, now, of your future? With what convictions must we turn our faces toward that; and in what temper must we deal with it? To these questions there is, I think, a three-fold answer, and when I have stated it I shall release you.

1. A Church exists, first of all, for worship; and in recognizing that fact, we are bound also to recognize that, if its faith is Catholic, its worship should be marked by the notes of that catholicity. The Reformation settlement stripped our mother Church of England of much that was a part of its most ancient inheritance; and that, apart from corrupt associations and the corrupted teaching of an unworthy ministry, had in it elements of august dignity, of singular beauty and of high edification. The temperamental differences of men will always lead them

to disagree as to the value of the external in worship; but unless we can show that the Founder of the Church dismissed all external rites and ceremonies from that first work of laying foundations of which the New Testament is the history, we must own that He has forever set His seal to the wise and right use of "the outward and visible" as the token and expression of "the invisible and spiritual"; and that it is at our peril that we disregard His teaching. The revolt, in the sixteenth and seventeenth centuries, from a ceremonialism which had grown barren of reverence, of decency often, and of all spiritual attributes, was natural and inevitable; but in many directions, and with tragic distinctiveness, as in the case of the Puritan iconoclasms and the absolute denudations of the Society of Friends, it went too far, and it destroyed too much. It was inevitable that a compensatory reaction should follow, and it did. Its influence has not ceased, and its effects are not yet at an end. Extravagances have marked this reaction, and are likely to continue to do so; but a wise temper will see in it something with which the Church may justly reckon, and to which you, my brethren of this parish, may wisely give your best consideration. Your worship need not be bald and dry and colorless in order to be evangelical or orthodox.

2. Again, another answer to the question which I have asked, as to our duty to the future, is to be found in our obligation to recognize the

nature and grounds of our divine message. The local interpretations of this are in one sense inevitable, in view of those temporary and transient influences to which I have already referred. During a large part of the history of this venerable parish, Churchmen connected with it, and other Churchmen around it, have been divided by dissensions, often marked by much heat and bitterness, between, *e.g.*, those who were " evangelical " and those who were "sacramentarians." With vehement protestation, on the one hand, and with a certain impatient scorn upon the other, they have impugned each other's intelligence, consistency, loyalty, and there are those still living who can remember the long and angry warfare which such differences involved.

As not unfrequently happens, both of them were right and each of them was wrong. The Church that held and holds them both, not, as her enemies are fond of affirming, in any poor spirit of compromise, but in a large and Christlike spirit of *comprehension*, held and holds the truth, alike, for which each of them was contending. That to some men they have seemed inconsistent and irreconcilable, is only because such persons have not been willing, or, as has been far oftener the case, able, to see them aright. That God is now bringing His Church to a larger and juster vision in this matter is a ground for devout thanksgiving. See to it, my brethren of this parish, that in the future ministries at that altar and in this pulpit, there is represented a teaching not less Catholic than that of the Church itself.

3. And yet, when you have secured both of them as elements in your future parochial life, you will not be complete. You will expect me, perhaps, to urge upon you, besides, the value of those various agencies, parish buildings, clubs, libraries, recreation rooms and the like, which, hereafter, will be recognized as one of the distinguishing notes in the Church's present aggressive life. I should certainly have no hesitation in doing so. Indeed, it is my duty to point out to a venerable parish like this, which possesses certain elements of material strength and permanency that are not common to all city churches, that it cannot expect to do the work which it ought to do in this neighborhood without adding to its equipment certain things— structures, organizations, mechanisms—which it is largely without. If it only aims to repeat, in the next hundred years, or in the next twenty years, the work that it has been doing during the last hundred, or the last twenty, then I should regard such a purpose as disclosing its utter unfitness for the trust which has been committed to its hands. You will hear from a certain type of divines, and sometimes also from laypeople of the same type, a fine scorn for what they call the mere humanitarianism of religion. This is the type of minister and the type of Christian that regard the Church as a sort of fetish, into the presence of which one must

crawl and supplicate its blessings at the hands of its sacerdotal representatives—or else go without those blessings. This is the type of teaching which practically regards the world as an irredeemable world, and the office of religion to be, mainly, to fit men as comfortably and safely as possible to get out of it. This is the type of Christian discipleship which holds its skirts away from vice and crime, and bids the Church tell the criminal what to expect in the next world, because it has not taken the trouble to show him how he ought to live in this. When it sneers at the institutional Church and seeks to pour contempt on the spirit of humanitarianism in the Church of God, in the name of Jesus Christ spew it out of your mouth, for it is none of His.

But, all the same, it is my duty to tell you that those modern means and agencies are *only* means and agencies, and no more. There is a distinct tendency to imagine that a parish house and Boys' Clubs and Girls' Friendly Guilds and the like will somehow energize, exorcise and administer, as it were by virtue of their own inherent force, in all those various relations in which the religion of Jesus Christ must touch and transform the life of man. They will do nothing of the sort. Multitudes of pastors today, are sighing and saying, "O if I only had a thousand, or a hundred thousand, or a million dollars (as the opportunity may be), how I would lift the life of this community!" Not at all, necessarily, or certainly, or even probably, my brother; unless all your more or less splendid and elaborate mechanism is shot through and through with the thrill of *personal service and sacrifice* made alive by the Holy Ghost! We are doing so much with machinery in these days, that it is not at all unnatural that men and women should expect to do with it the work of the Church. But it is a vain dream, and is doomed to inevitable disappointment. After you have built, and organized, and associated, still the wheels wait, as of old, for the "Living creature within the wheels," and God will not come back to New York until you and I make a highway for Him in the hearts of men in utter ignorance of whose lives, and in large indifference to their sorrows and perils, too many of us are living. When the great Apostle to the Gentiles, his heart bursting with passionate devotion to the love that had sought and found and regenerated him, strove to describe what his Master had been to him and done for him, he could do it in no other way so adequately as to say of Him, " The Son of God, who loved me and *gave himself for me.*" So Christ conquered. So must you and I! It is not culture, nor wealth, nor social leadership, nor political power that the Church needs to crave. What of these is worth having will come to it under the spell of its divine attraction, if it is fit to use them. But the genius of service, the spirit of sacrifice, the power of personal ministry, the graces made alive by the Holy Ghost, these alone can make the future of the Church's life, whether here or anywhere else, fruitful for God and man. And so, may He who can alone quicken and transform descend within these walls, and abide among this people, that, fired with love for Him, they may go forth into all the region round about, and win it for the Kingdom of our Lord, and of His Christ! Then "shall thine *age* be clear as the noonday; thou shalt shine forth; thou shalt be as the morning!"

Addresses made on Sunday Evening.

After Evening Prayer the speakers were introduced by the REV. CHARLES HENRY BABCOCK, D.D., minister-in-charge.

DR. BABCOCK: Two of the speakers whose names are on the programme cannot attend. The Rev Dr. Shipman, on account of illness, cannot be with us. The Rev. Dr. Rainsford, for the same reason, is compelled to be absent, being at present away under the care of his physician. Four parishes—Grace Church, Christ Church, St. George's Church, and St. Mark's Church—are united by ties of more than common interest. Because of the peculiarly close relations existing between Grace Church and St. Mark's Church, it seems to us that the first speaker this evening should be the REV. DR. HUNTINGTON, Rector of Grace Church.

ADDRESS OF DR. HUNTINGTON.

The Lion of St. Mark is not dead; no, nor even dormant. He is an old Lion, a century old; but to-day he rouses himself, asserts his right to be, and presently he will be heard from.

I have left a service in my own church and come around here to-night in compliance with the second of the two great commandments of the law, "Thou shalt love thy neighbor as thyself." Of the duties and privileges that attach to social life, no duties are more insistent, no privileges more precious than those entailed by neighborhood. It is as the representative of your neighbor, your younger sister Grace, that

I am here to-night. I come to bring you a message of good will and cheer, of congratulation that you and we are still here, on the same ground where we have been so long. The situation, ecclesiastical and religious, in this part of the City of New York appears to me to be full of interest. Lined along at intervals, like so many forts connected by an entrenchment, lined along on the north side of Tenth Street, stand three altars, and beside each altar a pulpit; three altars and three pulpits, walled in and roofed over—St. Mark's, Ascension, and Grace. Here they still are, after these many years; here they are, because in the Providence of God they have a work to do, a work which they may best do in concert with one another, with unity of purpose and unanimity of feeling.

There is often something strikingly significant about the names of churches, and I find a suggestion in the names of these three to which I have referred. They are named on different principles, these churches on the line of Tenth Street; it is not as if one was St. Philip's, and another St. John's, and another St. Peter's, but in each case there is a distinctive principle back of the name. This church, where we are keeping our anniversary, was named for a person, an evangelist, Ascension for a supernatural event, Grace for a spiritual power. If we analyze the sum total of religious activity and life, we shall find that what is most essential to Christianity is represented by these names.

The religion we profess is closely identified with personality. Jesus Christ committed none of His thoughts to writing. He planted them, instead, in the hearts of living men, men whom He sent forth as messengers, apostles, evangelists, to preach and to teach; and so long as His religion remains, what it has always been, a teaching religion, so long will men be needed to be the teachers—sanctified men, ordained men, men specially set apart for this one purpose, evangelists like St. Mark.

Not only so, but we have in Christianity that which links it indissolubly with history. The Gospel is a Gospel backed by facts. It is associated in our minds with certain great events of the past, the climax of which was that Ascension of the Christ which we are to commemorate this coming week. The Ascension was the crown of the Incarnation.

But, besides the Person and the event, Christianity demands the power, if the world is to get the full benefit of God's purpose; and so we have, beyond the Ascension and growing out of it, the coming of the Holy Ghost, the communication of power, and the name of this spiritual force is grace. Therefore it is that these three churches, St. Mark's, Ascension, Grace, stand as the emblems and the symbols of the three things most essential to the welfare of religion—the personal element, the doctrinal element, the energizing element. Let us, then, my dear brethren, standing firm on this our entrenched line, seek to embody and illustrate, by our united action, the principles which our three names suggest. Let us work shoulder to shoulder, heart to heart, carrying on our pastoral work with diligence, teaching the truth with fidelity, ministering the Spirit with power.

And so I end where I began, with a message of good will and neighborly affection. St. Mark, you remember, is the patron saint of Venice, that memorable city which was to the Europe of its day what New York is to the America of the present, its great commercial capital. The legend of Venice, alike civic and sacred in its character, runs thus: *Pax tibi, Marce, Evangelista Meus.* In the spirit of that venerable motto I come to you to-night, and say in Grace's name, "Peace be with you, Mark, my Evangelist."

DR. BABCOCK: It may not be known to all who are present that this church stands on the oldest continuous church site in New York. Before St. Mark's was built here, the spot was occupied for one hundred years by what is known as the Old Dutch Church. For this reason, I take pleasure in introducing the REV. DR. COE, senior minister of the Collegiate Dutch Church of this city, as the next speaker.

ADDRESS OF DR. COE.

The sight of a minister of the Dutch Church in this place may seem strange to the men of this generation. But it is a pleasant reminder of the ancient history of this spot and of the friendly relations which subsisted here in former times between the Churches of England and Holland. More than two hundred years have passed away since Gov. Peter Stuyvesant died, and was buried in the plot of ground where this church now stands. His great farm has long since been swallowed up in the growth of the city which he once ruled in a somewhat despotic way. Even his famous pear-tree, which was still standing at the corner of Thirteenth Street and Third Avenue when I was a boy, and which I used daily to pass on my way to school, disappeared many years ago. But you have not forgotten the fact that St. Mark's Church occupies the site of the chapel which he built in his "bouwerie." Here he employed one of the earliest Dutch schoolmasters, Van Hoboocken by name, to hold religious services by reading the Scriptures and the Creeds. And here Domine Selyns, then a Dutch minister in Brooklyn and afterward pastor of the Dutch Church in New York, was engaged by him to preach from time to time to his household and his forty or fifty negro slaves. The governor was a religious man, even if he was rather narrow-minded and passionate. Almost his first official act had been to secure the passage of an ordinance for the better observance of the Sabbath. And the best way to promote the proper observance of the Sabbath seemed to him (not unnaturally) to be to compel everybody to attend the Dutch Church. This he accordingly proceeded to do by dint of sharp pains and penalties. But the spirit of tolerance, which had so remarkably characterized the people of Holland, was too strong in the colony to permit this arbitrary exercise of power, and soon brought upon Stuyvesant the rebuke of the authorities at home.

With the surrender of the city to the English in 1664, the control of it passed, of course, into other hands. English colonists came in larger numbers, and with them came the Church of England. But there are two things connected with this which deserve to be remembered to the credit of both parties. One is, that, by the articles of surrender, the Dutch were not to be molested in their religious doctrines or policy, or in their titles to their places of worship. They retained full and undisputed possession of these, including even their stone chapel in the fort. The other is, that as the chaplain of the victorious English forces had no place in which to celebrate the English service, the Dutch offered him for this purpose the use of that chapel, when they were not using it themselves. It was under these circumstances that the Episcopal liturgy was first read in New York, and this friendly arrangement continued for twenty-nine years.

It is pleasant also to remember that when the Rev. Mr. Vesey, who had been sent for ordination to England, was inducted into office as the first rector of Trinity Church, two Dutch ministers took part in the service, which was conducted in Latin, and subscribed the record of it. The service itself was held in the Dutch Church in Garden Street (now Exchange Place), where, for several months, the English congregation continued to worship, till their own edifice was completed. This hospitality was courteously reciprocated during the Revolution, when the Garden Street Church was transformed by the British into a hospital, and the use of St. George's Chapel was offered by the Episcopalians to the Dutch congregation, who worshipped there till their own edifice was restored to them.

New York is to-day neither a Dutch nor an English, but a distinctly American city. All races are mingled in its vast population. All forms of worship and of religious belief subsist here peaceably together. But it seems as if there should be something more than peace— there should be heartiest good-will and cooperation between those two branches of the Church to which the earliest settlers in this city belonged. And such mutual respect and kind feeling have most happily continued to the present time. The invitation of your vestry, by which I have been honored, to represent the Dutch Church at this service, is an evidence of this, which we on our part cordially reciprocate. It is not surprising that we have come to be outnumbered by the adherents of religious bodies of English origin and traditions, or that many names once associated with our Church are now honorably identified with yours. But an unbroken line of succession connects us with the beginnings of Christian worship on this island. And if we are still true to the evangelical doctrine which was preached in the fort by your ministers and by ours, we are also still loyal to the traditions of Christian comity and fellowship which have come down from those far-distant days. We rejoice in your growth and your increasing prosperity. We rejoice in the tenacity with which you hold positions like this, which were once far out in the country and are now equally far down town. We rejoice in the steady and noble work which St. Mark's Church has done in all the century now ended and is still doing at the present moment.

In some respects, the Dutch Church and the Episcopal Church are in closer sympathy with one another than is generally realized. We, too, are accustomed to the use of liturgical forms. We are even required to use them on special occasions, and the whole spirit of our worship is distinctly liturgical. We repeat from time to time the same prayers which you also employ, some of which are derived, as you know, from the liturgies composed or arranged by the great Swiss reformers. The ancient creeds are as fa miliar to us as to you. And your doctrinal formulas are not less Calvinistic than ours. Differing as we do in our forms of church government and in some other things also, we are one with you in our profound reverence for the Bible, in our high regard for the authority and significance of the Sacraments, in our observance of the chief festivals of the Christian year, and in our respect for the historic unity and development of the Church. It was not without reason that the national Churches of Holland and England felt themselves drawn toward each other in the olden time, or that the English governors of this colony showed a marked consideration for the religious opinions and usages to which the sturdy Dutchmen clung with a firmness that has sometimes been thought to resemble obstinacy. And we of this later day, who pride ourselves on our more refined manners and our more liberal views, ought surely to show ourselves no less truly catholic and Christian than our fathers were two centuries ago. Free from all jealousy, all self-seeking, and all self-adulation, we shall, if the spirit of the Master is in us, join hands and hearts in the great work to which He has called us. And as I bring you tonight the greetings and the congratulations of the ancient Dutch Church of this city, now more than than two hundred and seventy years old, it is with the prayer that God may speed the day when, not we alone, but all who profess and call themselves Christians, shall be still more closely united in the bonds of a common faith and the consecration of a common service. May the blessing of the Lord our God be upon you in the future as it has been in the past.

DR. BABCOCK: St. Mark's Church has reached out in various directions, not merely in ecclesiastical, but also in academic ways.

The time was, many years ago, when the rector of St. Mark's Church was president of Columbia College; and, on account of that double service, it is my privilege to introduce this evening PROF. VAN AMRINGE, Dean of Columbia University.

ADDRESS OF DEAN VAN AMRINGE.

I bring to you this evening the congratulations of Columbia College and University.

It is interesting to note that the corner-stone of the first edifice for St. Mark's was laid by a graduate of the first class in King's College—as Columbia was known before the Revolution—the Right Rev. Samuel Provoost, first Bishop of New York; and that when the building was ready for occupancy, it was consecrated by Bishop Provoost, and the sermon on the occasion was preached by the Rev. Benjamin Moore, who was also a graduate of King's College, was twice president of his *alma mater*, and became the second Bishop of this diocese. The first active rector of this parish, though not the first in name, was the Rev. William Harris, who, while rector, became president of Columbia, and served her faithfully as such for eighteen years. He was the immediate successor in that office of Bishop Moore, during the latter part of whose term great activity prevailed in the councils of the College. The courses of education and discipline, which had come down without great change from pre-revolutionary times, needed revision. They were thoroughly revised just as

Bishop Moore retired; and the question of his successor was thereby rendered difficult to decide, and created at the time a great deal of feeling. A considerable and influential party desired the election of Dr. John M. Mason, who had been prominent in the movement for revision and was largely instrumental in bringing it about. He was a learned and able man, of decided character, and distinguished among other things for his eloquence in the pulpit. He was not, however, a Churchman; and inasmuch as Columbia then held, and still holds, a valuable part of its real estate as a gift from Trinity Church, on the express condition that the president for the time being shall be a communicant of the Church, it was impracticable, without danger of great loss, to make Dr. Mason president. A compromise was therefore effected, by which an officer styled the provost was provided for, and to this officer were given powers larger and more important than those of the president —and Dr. Mason was chosen for that office.

It was evident that the gentleman who should assume the presidency must needs have unusual qualities of mind and temper to enable him to discharge his duties with credit to himself and without embarrassment to the institution. This difficult position Dr. Harris was, in 1811, invited to fill, and, happily, he accepted the responsibility. His dignity of character and spirituality of mind were so great, his consideration for those with whom he was associated, officers and students, was so constant and kind, he was so scholarly, so wise and tactful, that the desired changes were effected without friction, and the College had full advantage of the services of both provost and president. This dual arrangement was terminated in 1816, and Dr. Harris had, thenceforward, for thirteen years, full and sole charge as head of the College. He had under his jurisdiction, as students, many men who subsequently became distinguished, and they, one and all, esteemed him highly. One of them, the late eminent classicist and professor, Charles Anthon, whose brother was rector here for twenty-five years, deemed the period of Dr. Harris's presidency the halcyon time of the College; and another, the late Rev. Dr. Benjamin I. Haight, spoke of "the honored and beloved President Harris"; and said: "He was a remarkable man, not so much for any one feature of his character, as for the happy combination of the several qualities of mind and heart which go to make the effective guide, teacher, and friend of young men."

Columbia was especially fortunate in having such a man for president, and sends cordial messages of good will and good wishes to St. Mark's, that had in him so admirable a spiritual guide; and she sends these hearty greetings not only on account of the connection of which I have spoken, but also because in her opinion there is no association so necessary for the good of the individual and the welfare of the State, as a close alliance between an institution of learning and a Christian Church like this; because purely intellectual accomplishment, which it is the business, in part, of a university to cultivate, is not necessarily of and by itself an advantage to a man or to mankind, but may, on the contrary, be a serious detriment, unless it is joined with the sterling character that can come only from a firm and devout belief in the enduring principles and the vital doctrines which the Church teaches and impresses upon all her children.

DR. BABCOCK: With due regard to proportion in education, St. Mark's Church has been interested in a practical way with theological as well as academical learning. The present occupant of the Chair of Ecclesiastical History in the General Theological Seminary has kindly consented to address us this evening. I introduce the REV. DR. RICHEY as the last speaker.

ADDRESS OF DR. RICHEY.

Christianity has had given to it a double mission in the world. Our Lord said to His disciples, "Ye are the salt of the earth." He means to say that Christianity is intended to be in society of the nature of a productive energy or power, which is to give fertility and life. I could not help thinking, as my reverend brother was telling of the end of Peter Stuyvesant, on whose soil we have all met together to-night, that in his character—that good old Dutch and sterling Calvinistic character, which came with him and his countrymen to the work they undertook to do—there appeared a strong sense of moral obligation. In them all that strength and force of character and power was manifested, and in Peter Stuyvesant it was what men would now call a dominating character. It is to these men that we owe the fertility which made productive the barren soil in which Christianity at that time struck such deep root. All honor to the men, and all honor to the system under which they were educated and brought up! and we can but return insistently the good words which we have heard to-night.

Columbia College on the one hand, and the General Theological Seminary on the other, both owe to St. Mark's Church, through the characters of Dr. Harris and Peter Gerard Stuyvesant, much of that influence and power that I am called upon more especially to present.

In the year 1835 the City of New York was visited by a fire that was almost as destructive and overwhelming as the great fire which brought the city of Chicago to ruin some years ago. At that time there was a young man who was the Rector of St. Mark's Church, Orange, watching the devastating flame as it spread over the whole heaven and lit up the sky. He came into New York next day; and on the Sunday after he was asked to take the place of Dr. Taylor, then Rector of Grace Church, and to preach the sermon, because he was himself a man capable of the inspiration of mighty sympathy, as well as a man of intellect. And that sermon has associations, not only with Grace Church and with this parish and with the General Theological Seminary, but it illustrated something which I think is remarkable to see. After his sermon, one of the parishioners said, "I should like, Dr. Whittingham, to borrow that sermon." He answered, in his impetuous way, "I never lend my sermons to anybody." But his solicitor said, "I must have that sermon." To which Dr. Whittingham replied, "I wont lend it to you, but I will give it to you." And the parishioner said, "I will give you $20,000 then."

When Peter Gerard Stuyvesant endowed the Chair of Ecclesiastical History in the General Theological Seminary, he nominated Dr. Hawks, who was his personal friend, to fill it. Dr. Hawks could not accept the position; and it was then bestowed upon the man who preached the sermon for which he got $20,000. He was the first professor on the endowment of Mr. Stuyvesant that has since, in the intellectual sphere, represented St. Mark's Church.

Now I want to say to you something of two of the men that have occupied that sphere in your behalf.

Dr. Whittingham is an example of the man who from the earliest years had the vocation of scholarship. It began, so to speak, in his childhood. It came from a source which, after all, is the source of great moral power (as was said by my predecessor) in this world below. When asked by his examiners, "Where were you educated?" he said, "I was educated by my mother." " But," he was asked, "who taught you Latin and Greek and Hebrew?" To which he replied, " I learned them from my mother." Now, that was the secret of the moral energy which the man drank in, and became a power of life in every fibre of his intellectual being. He was four years only in the Seminary; but in those four years he left a mark which never can be effaced. It was there that he met constantly the young men who gathered round about him. During those four years his influence was felt, not only in the Seminary, but on literature—in such a way as it has never been since felt in New York. There was organized at this time what was known as " The Press." A number of laymen took upon them the task of distribution, and he established and directed the movement. His influence went out everywhere—that wonderful influence which led him to be elected Bishop four years after.

The other person I have in mind was one who was my own dear personal friend. He was a noble illustration of how God distributes His gifts to the sons of men. Dr. Whittingham was impetuous, filled with energy and enthusiasm. Dr. Mahan was of the nature of a mystic, one of the deepest and profoundest minds that the American Church has ever known. He was a man of a retiring, noble nature. He went for a number of years to the General Convention, and never made a speech, nor opened his mouth. Dr. Hawks once paid him a great compliment.

When we were in danger of a division in the Church at the time of the Civil War, it was Dr. Mahan who got up in the Convention and made a speech, of which Dr. Hawks was so generous as to say, that if he could make such a speech he would consider it the great achievement of his life. Dr. Mahan was as modest as he was great, and it was hard to draw him out. Sometimes he would get so lost in mystic dreams that his wife would have to tell him, "You have got to preach to-night in such and such a church." And sometimes, when he went to church, instead of attending to outward things he would be thinking of his sermon. At St. Peter's Church he once made a great commotion, quiet as he was. He was kneeling at the altar, and for a time forgot that he was in the church; and when he was to pronounce the Absolution there was a dead silence. After a while the dear, good man got up and, instead of the Absolution, he pronounced the Benediction: then he went down on his knees again, as though nothing at all had taken place.

Seventy-five years ago, if you had come to see us in Chelsea Square, you would have had to enter through an apple orchard. Now the apple orchard is gone; but we have in its place a magnificent, charming close and a lovely chapel, which is the work of the present dean, Dr. Hoffman.

It gives me great pleasure as your missionary to appear among you to-night, and let me add, dear brethren : " Come to Chelsea Square, make it—as Columbia College is in its own sphere—an intellectual centre, to scatter its light all over the world."

THE NEW YORK
PUBLIC LIBRARY.

ASTOR, LENOX AND
TILDEN FOUNDATIONS.

ST. MARK'S CHURCH,
MAY 9TH, 1899.

Address on Tuesday, May 9th, by the Reverend the Rector of Trinity Church, Dr. Dix.

A citizen of New York, if he be a person of sensibility, with such reverence for the past as is becoming in mortal man, has cause for sadness when considering how little veneration for old and time-honored objects is to be found in this community. True, there are those in whom the sentiment is not dead, but they are few in number compared with the multitude of pushing, driving, boisterous folk who deem it weakness to cherish the old, and continually clamor for something new.

So far as I remember, there is in this city only one complete surviving relic of the pre-revolutionary age, our dear old St. Paul's Chapel, on Broadway and Vesey Street; but it has required constant vigilance and determination on the part of the corporation to which the sacred fane belongs to save it from destruction; for there are barbarians among us who covet the site for business purposes, and would rejoice to see the edifice, the adjacent cemetery, and the pretty garden plot, now blooming with leafage and flowers, buried beneath the ponderous pile of several more of those repulsive and horrible structures which reduce our streets to mere cañons, through which the wind roars, and into whose depths no sunbeam makes its way.

All about us is in flux; nothing, or next to nothing, survives; while no suspicion of detriment to character and morals seems to disturb the general conscience of a people indifferent to the past, and pushing on with new ventures, new fads, new experiments, to result, no mortal can say in what. Of such are they who are now at work, not far off, hacking at our beautiful and historic Palisades, and blowing off the cliffs with dynamite to save a few cents a load on stone for road beds; or those still worse enemies of the community who would convert the cataract of Niagara into a machine for running a vast electric plant.

To one who watches the trend of which I speak, it is matter for rejoicing, when occasionally, as in the present instance, he is invited to celebrate an instance of preservation, and not of destruction; when an object is to be seen which has lived through ten decades of years, without being pulled down or swept away; of which, still better, we may venture a hopeful prediction that it will last a hundred years more, steadily and successfully resisting vandal assault, and keep in 1999 the two-hundredth anniversary, as now it keeps, in 1899, the one-hundredth. With gladness, with a sense of relief, with good will, do we come, to make merry and be glad with the Corporation and Congregation of this old Church of St. Mark's-in-the-Bowery, on this centennial day. Long may these walls stand! and palsied be the arm that shall be first lifted to cast them down!

I deem it an honour to have been chosen to prepare an address suitable to the day. When I recall the sermon, mainly historical, preached in this church by the Rev. Henry Anthon, D.D., May 4, 1845, on occasion of the fiftieth anniversary of the laying of the corner-stone, and published by request of the Vestry; and the historic discourse delivered on Sunday, April 21, 1895, by the Rev. J. H. Rylance, D.D., then Rector, and now *Rector-emeritus*, on the hundredth anniversary of the same event, it seems as if a third paper of this class were hardly needed, and that it might have been better for the Vestry to have reprinted either or both of those very interesting and valuable monographs.*

But since they have deemed it good to invite a repetition of the story, I will do what I can to meet the request.

And, first, to speak of the quaint name of your parish, "St. Mark's Church-in-the-Bowery." It

---

* " Parish Annals." A sermon giving Historical Notices of St. Mark's Church in the Bowery, New York (from A.D. 1795 to A.D. 1845). Delivered in said Church, May 4, 1845, by Henry Anthon, D.D., Rector of the same. Published by the request of the Vestry. New York: Stanford & Swords, No. 139 Broadway. 1845. 12mo, pp. 58.

" The Centennial of St. Mark's Church, New York City." A Discourse delivered on Sunday, April 21, 1895, by the Rector, J. H. Rylance, D.D. Published by the Vestry. New York: Thomas Whittaker, Bible House. 1895. Small 4to, pp. 23.

has an old-time flavour which is refreshing; it recalls to our thoughts St. Martin's-in-the-Fields, and St. Mary-le-Bow; there comes to the eye, as we hear the title, a pleasant glint of light from the far-off days of New Amsterdam. By a Bouwerie was meant, in those days, a gentleman's country seat, a cultured and inhabited plot of ground as distinguished from the rough and wild plantation.* Outside of the town of New Amsterdam, the well-to-do and, for that time, opulent burghers had their Bouweries, or country seats, from which our well-known street, the Bowery, took its name. One of those pleasant places, large in extent, belonged to the notable Peter Stuyvesant, the last of the Dutch governors.† According to the old chronicles, the municipal authorities of New Amsterdam gave permission to establish a hamlet near the governor's Bouwerie; and when the tavern, blacksmith's shop, and other buildings had been provided, the governor, being a God-fearing man, and a staunch adherent to his Church, built what Dr. Rylance describes as "a modest rural chapel" in his park, probably for the accommodation of his family and the few residents in the neighborhood, that Almighty God might be duly worshipped according to the faith and ceremonies of the Reformed Protestant Dutch Church of Holland, then established here by law. In that chapel Harman Van Hoboocken,

---

* O'Callaghan. "History of New Netherlands," Vol. II., p. 291.
† For an account of Gov. Stuyvesant's Bouwerie, see John R. Brodhead's "History of New York," First Period, p. 681.

the city chorister and schoolmaster, used to read service on Sundays;* but in the year 1660, the governor, desiring to make better provision for the services, secured the aid of Dominie Henricus Selyns, the minister in charge of the congregation at Breukelen (now Brooklyn), engaging to pay 250 guilders toward his salary, provided that he would agree, in addition to his other duties, to preach at the Bouwerie on Sunday evenings.

The chapel, now become a place of considerable importance, stood partly on the site occupied by the church in which we are assembled. Mr. Benjamin R. Winthrop, after a careful study of the subject, reached the conclusion that the western gable of the old church must have stood ten or twelve feet from the eastern gable of the present edifice.†

Gov. Stuyvesant's official life was cut short, A.D. 1664, upon the occupation of the town by the British. In 1672 his mortal life also ended, and his body was buried beneath the little chapel which he had built in his park. After his death, it appears to have lost its proprietary character, and to have been cared for by the Church authorities, until another and a greater change came. More than one hundred years later, on the site of the old chapel, your church was founded, through the efforts of an-

---

* "History of the School of the Collegiate Reformed Dutch Church in the City of New York." New York, 1883, pp. 23 and 29.

† See a paper read before the New York Historical Society, Feb. 4, 1862.

other Peter Stuyvesant, great-grandson of the governor, who was then a member of the Corporation of Trinity Church.

You are, perhaps, aware that in those early days there was a slow but steady drift of the Dutch into the Church of England, accelerated as Trinity, the mother of churches, gained in influence and spiritual power; the history which I am narrating gives an instance of the movement and its important results.

I am glad to think that the honour of founding this parish belongs to old Trinity.

It was not, like St. George's and St. Paul's, a chapel of the parish, but an independent corporation. Up to that time each new church of ours on Manhattan Island had been erected by Trinity Church as a chapel of ease. The question whether the proposed church to be built on the site of the chapel in the Bouwerie could be made a church distinct from Trinity parish was carefully considered by a committee, consisting of Messrs. Richard Harison and Alexander Hamilton, and upon a favorable report by them measures were taken to carry out the design.* The following extracts from the Minutes of the Vestry of Trinity relate the further progress of the movement:

At a meeting of the Corporation of Trinity Church, held at Trinity Church on Monday, the 8th of July, 1793.

* See Berrian's "History," p. 188. The opinion of Messrs. Harison and Hamilton is mentioned in the Minutes of Trinity Vestry of April 9, 1798, and a copy of the document might probably be found in the parish archives.

Present:
The Right Rev. Bishop Provost, Rector,
Robert Watts, Churchwarden.
VESTRYMEN:

Hugh Gaine,	David M. Clarkson,	William S. Johnson,
Peter Stuyvesandt,	James Farquhar,	William Laight,
John Jones,	Anthony L. Bleecker,	Thomas Barrow,
Charles Startin,	John Lewis,	Augustus Van Horne,
Andrew Hamersly,	Nicholas Carmer,	Richard Harison.

Mr. Stuyvesandt's offer respecting an Episcopal Church to be built upon his land—towards which he engages to give £800 and a lot of land 150 feet in width and 190 feet in length, was taken into consideration. Thereupon,

Resolved: That this Board do accept of the same and will take measures for building a church accordingly, as soon as the situation of the Corporation will admit thereof, and that Messrs. Stuyvesandt, Gaine and Jones be a committee to procure proper plans for the building, and to enquire what aids can be obtained from well-disposed persons towards the same.

At a meeting of the Corporation of Trinity Church, held at Trinity Church, on Monday, the nineteenth day of January, 1795.
Present: The Rt. Rev. Bishop Provoost,* Rector.
Robert Watts, Churchwarden.
VESTRYMEN.

William S. Johnson,	John Jones,	Charles Startin,
David M. Clarkson,	William Laight,	Hugh Gaine,
Andrew Hamersly,	James Farquhar,	Jacob Le Roy,
Hubert Van Wagenen,	Anthony L. Bleecker,	Richard Harison.
Augustus Van Horne,	Thomas Barrows,	
Nicholas Carmer,	Peter Stuyvesandt,	

Resolved: That this Corporation will raise the sum of £5,000 for building a church on the land of Peter Stuyvesandt, Esq., in conformity with his proposals, and that if the lots already directed to be sold are not sufficient for that purpose and the other purposes specified in the Report, the Committee of Leases consider of such others as may be proper to be disposed of; and,

Resolved: That Messrs. Carmer, Gaine, Van Horne and Stuyvesandt be a committee to superintend the building of the said church.†

* It will be observed that the Bishop's name appears in the record of July 8, 1793, with two o's, and here with three. He himself spelled it in different ways, sometimes Provost and sometimes Provoost.

† Minute Books of Trinity Church and St. Mark's Church; also Berrian's "History of Trinity Church," pp. 186-87.

The corner-stone of St. Mark's Church was laid on the twenty-fifth day of April, 1795, by the Rt. Rev. Samuel Provoost, Bishop of New York, and rector of Trinity. The question, what should be the status of the new congregation, was still unsettled. In the minutes of Trinity Church Corporation, January 9, 1797, we find the following record:

> The committee appointed to consider what measures it will be proper to adopt with respect to St. Mark's Church report as their opinion that the said church should be finished in a decent manner by the end of next summer, and that, as it would be inexpedient to increase the number of churches to be supported by this Corporation, measures should be taken by the advice of counsel for organizing a corporation to consist of Protestant Episcopalians, disposed to form a corporation there, or for placing them otherwise in a situation to receive farther assistance from this Corporation in the most safe and convenient method, due regard being always had to their union with the Protestant Episcopal Church in the United States. Thereupon,
>
> *Resolved:* That the Board agree to the above report, and that the counsel of the Corporation be requested to consider of and state a proper plan for carrying the same into execution.

Meanwhile progress was made with the building, which was completed in 1799, and consecrated on the ninth day of May in that year by Bishop Provoost, the preacher on the occasion being the Rev. Dr. Benjamin Moore.

On the nineteenth of August following Messrs. Peter Stuyvesandt,* Martin Hoffman, George Rapelje, Francis Bayard Winthrop, Mangle Minthorne and William A. Hardenbrook were appointed trustees to hold the property until a corporation could be formed and a

---
* In the old records of Trinity Parish the name is always spelt thus.

parish constituted. Mr. Stuyvesandt was chosen president, and Mr. Hoffman clerk.

At a meeting held September 24th these trustees took order for an election of two churchwardens and eight vestrymen, to be chosen by the persons composing the congregation of the church; and to that end a sale of pews was held, October 2d, the purchasers thus becoming corporators of the new parish.*

Pews Nos. 41 and 76 were reserved for the rector, churchwardens and vestry; No. 9 was presented to Mr. Stuyvesandt, free of rent, for five years. No. 108 was reserved, to quote the record, "for the governor and other respectable characters who may occasionally attend divine service in the church"; a gratifying testimonial to the probable respectability of chief magistrates of the State, in the current judgment of the day.

The first vestry was elected October 18th, consisting of Peter Stuyvesandt and Francis Bayard Winthrop, as wardens, and Gilbert Colden Willett, William A. Hardenbrook, William Ogden, Nicholas William Stuyvesant, Martin Hoffman, Mangle Minthorne, George Turnbull and James Cummings, vestrymen.

Easter Tuesday was fixed as the day for the annual election for churchwardens and vestrymen, and the legal name of the Corporation was adopted as "The Rector, Churchwardens, and

---

*Thirty-seven pews were sold on a five years' lease, at from 30 to 140 shillings per annum, making a total of £96 10s., or about $242.

Vestrymen of the Protestant Episcopal Church of St. Mark's in the Bowery in the City of New York."

A report of all these proceedings was made to the vestry of Trinity Church, and is acknowledged in the minutes of their meeting of November 10th.

At the first vestry meeting, held November 5, 1799, Mr. Stuyvesant was elected Clerk, and Mr. Hoffman, Treasurer. Luke Kip was appointed Sexton, and on the thirtieth of January next ensuing, the Rev. John Callaghan, of South Carolina, was called to the rectorship at a salary of £500, equivalent to $1,250.

Financial difficulties are apt to embarrass all undertakings in the line of church extension; it was so in the case of the new parish. The income from pew rents was less than $300, while the annual expenses, including the salary of the rector, and those of sexton, clerk, etc., were estimated at $1,900. As was the custom, in those days, recourse was had to the Corporation of Trinity Church, who received a great number of petitions from that quarter, and cheerfully responded to them. It is evident from the records that the burden of founding and establishing the new parish fell mainly on our churchwardens and vestrymen, so that St. Mark's, though not a chapel, may fairly be regarded as a child of the old mother. On the ninth of November, 1801, the question of an endowment for St. Mark's being under consideration, it was decided to make a grant of thirty lots, being a part of the Church Estate received from Queen Anne, and the following action was taken :

Resolved: That this Board approve the report of their committee, and that the lots selected be conveyed to St. Mark's Church whenever the counsel of the Corporation shall devise a mode whereby this Corporation shall be secured from any future demands or interference of the members of said church, and that in the meantime this Corporation do agree to pay to said church £300 per annum in addition to the former grant of £200 per annum, to commence on the twenty-fifth day of March next, and that when the above mentioned conveyance shall be made all arrears of rent which shall be due on the lots to be conveyed shall be secured to this Corporation.

The grant was confirmed June 9, 1802, at which time your vestry executed a deed of release of any right, title, interest, or future demand to the estate and property of the grantors.*

In addition to this liberal grant of thirty lots of land, many other grants, gifts and donations were subsequently made by Trinity to the new parish. It must also be remembered that Mr. Peter Stuyvesant gave liberally to the same object, conveying to the vestry a lot 56x95 feet on what is now Eleventh Street, as the site of a parsonage, and thereafter presenting them with another plot on the same street, 242x190 feet, for a cemetery. In acknowledgment of these handsome benefactions, on the part of Mr. Stuyvesant, the gift of Pew No. 9 to him was made perpetual. Further aid came from Trinity in 1807 by way of a contribution of $500 toward the completing and strengthening of the tower, although they declined a request that they

*A copy of this quit-claim deed is given in full in the Appendix.

should expend a much larger sum and put a spire upon it. The gift of a bell from the tower of St. Paul's Chapel was also made about that time. There were several bells in St. Paul's; this was known as the smaller bell. It was loaned by your vestry to St. Clement's Church in 1837 and in 1859 the gift was made permanent.

When first completed the church was without steeple, balustrade or portico, nor was there any building in the rear. In 1800 the grounds were enclosed. In 1804 it was resolved to fence in the burial ground with "neat palings in front and boards in their original state on the sides and rear." In 1804, also, the pews in the gallery were completed, and in 1806 a tower or belfry, without spire, appears to have been added. In the following year permission was granted for the construction of vaults for the burial of the dead. The body of General Petrus Stuyvesant still lay in a vault beneath the old chapel: that vault was now taken in, and inclosed in the wall of the new church, where it remains to this day, with a suitable memorial tablet visible from the outer churchyard walk.

An organ was placed in the church in 1823 at a cost of $1,150, and between the years 1826 and 1829 the steeple was built at a cost of $5,000, Messrs. Thomson and Town being the architects. In 1834 the building in the rear containing Sunday-school rooms was erected; in 1835 a vane and clock were added to the furnishings of the steeple, and in 1836 the edifice was greatly beautified and improved by the erection of the portico looking to the south and east. The iron railing which still encloses the churchyard was placed there in 1838, about which time also the interior of the church was repaired, and to some extent altered, the old pews and the chancel furniture being given away to other parishes to which such donations were valuable. In 1840 a new rectory was built on the corner of Second Avenue and Tenth Street, and a second organ was purchased in 1847. In 1858 the present portico, together with the cornice and balustrade on the roof, were erected, and finally, in 1888, another organ, the third up to that time, was put in.

From these statistics relating to the building let us proceed to consider the rectors of the parish, who, from its foundation to the present day, have laboured here for the faith of the Gospel and the edification of the household of Christ. It has been stated already, that on the thirtieth of January, 1800, the Rev. John Callaghan, of South Carolina, was called to the rectorship. In the records of May 8th of the same year we find an announcement of this unfortunate gentleman's untimely death. While on a visit to his relations in Charleston, he was thrown from a carriage, and died of the injury received in that fatal accident, which occurred April 14, 1800, only two months and a half after his call to be rector of St. Mark's. After the death of Mr. Callaghan, the office remained vacant nearly two years. Invitations were extended to the Rev. Messrs. John H. Hobart, Philander Chase, Cave Jones and Theodore Dehon, but were successively declined. It is worthy of note that of these gentlemen, three, Hobart, Chase and Dehon, subsequently became Bishops.

On the third of December, 1801, the Rev. William Harris, D.D., was elected rector, and inducted February 6, 1802. Dr. Harris served for more than fourteen years. In 1811 he was elected President of Columbia College. In consequence of the increasing burden of his duties in that important office, he resigned the rectorship of St. Mark's, and preached his farewell sermon November 24, 1816. Ten days later, December 3d, the Rev. William Creighton, D.D., was called as rector, and held office until May 5, 1836, on which date he resigned, withdrawing to another field of work. Dr. Creighton is well remembered by us, your elders, as one of the best and loveliest men of his day; and no one who witnessed it can forget the scene in the convention of the Diocese of New York, in 1851, when he, having been almost unanimously elected to be Provisional Bishop, declined the office, the tears streaming down his face, as he uttered the cry, "Dear brethren, I cannot be your Bishop!" There*

---

* Dr. Creighton, having been president of every convention for many preceding years, was nominated as Provisional Bishop, and received a majority of the clerical vote on two ballots at the Special Convention of 1850. (See "Journal," p. 41, *et seq*.) In

was, as many knew, a cause sufficient to account for that emotion, and to move to deepest sympathy with our noble and great-hearted friend and father, whose soul was wrung by a conflict between a personal duty, arising out of heavy domestic affliction, and that other duty to God and the Church to which the conscientious priest hardly knows how to assign its place in the shock of rival claims.

Among the incidents of Dr. Creighton's rectorship was the endowment of a chair in the General Theological Seminary, by Mr. Peter G. Stuyvesant. In 1835 he made a gift of $25,000 for that purpose, the chair to be known as the "St. Mark's Church in the Bowery Professorship of Ecclesiastical History." Dr. Clement C. Moore, of pleasant and delightsome memory, scholar, poet, instructor, had previously given the land upon which the noble buildings of the Seminary now stand, among the most conspicuous ornaments of the city in point of architectural effect, and still more interesting to the Churchman as the home of sound theology and sacred learning.

Dr. Creighton was succeeded, December 17, 1836, by the Rev. Henry Anthon, D.D., who held office until the day of his death, January 5, 1861. When called to the rectorship of St. Mark's in the Bowery, he was an assistant-minister of Trinity

1851 he was nominated again and elected. (See "Journal," pp. 96-8.) His address is given on page 99, and his letter of declination is in the "Journal" of 1852, pp. 77-9.

Church, and stationed at St. John's Chapel. I have an impression that things were not running with perfect smoothness when the offer came, and that the change was opportune ; but those matters are lost in a friendly haze, where they may best remain.

During his rectorship the fiftieth anniversary of the laying of the corner-stone of this church was duly celebrated, May 4, 1845, and, as has already been stated, he delivered a historical sermon appropriate to the day and enriched with valuable notes.

The Rev. Alexander H. Vinton, D.D., the fifth rector, was elected March 5, 1861, and held office until October 15, 1869. Many important advances were made during his term of office. The Anthon Memorial Church had been erected by the vestry of St. Mark's in 1859; in 1866 a chapel known as St. Mark's Chapel was founded on Avenue A; the present building was subsequently erected in 1884 by Mr. Rutherford Stuyvesant as a memorial to his wife, a lovely lady of an honoured and illustrious house. The church grounds were extended by purchase of additional land on Second Avenue, and the interior of the church was painted and otherwise improved.

Dr. Vinton resigned the rectorship October 15, 1869. An invitation to succeed him having been declined by the Rev. William R. Huntington, D.D., the Rev. Joseph H. Rylance, D.D., was elected January 27, 1871. He accepted the position, entering upon his duties March, 1871, and serving until Advent, 1898, when he was made *rector emeritus*, and retired from the administration of the parish which he served with distinguished ability and devotion for more than twenty-six years.

As is the case in our older parishes, many personal recollections are interwoven with the official records. It is so here: those records shine with well-known names.

By way of introduction to the mortuary record, I may observe that the building was put in mourning for six weeks, in July and August, 1804, on the occasion of the sudden and dreadful death of that prince among the men of his time, Alexander Hamilton, to whom may be applied without change or reserve the well-known lines:

"Clarum et venerabile nomen
Gentibus, et multum nostrae quod profuit urbi."

The first wardens of the parish were lineal descendants of Governors Stuyvesant and Winthrop. Among the original pewholders were Hugh Gaine, one of the earliest and best printers of the city, and Gen. Horatio Gates. Notable among the wardens and vestrymen were Col. Nicholas Fish, of Revolutionary fame, Gideon Lee, once Mayor of New York, Jacob Lorillard, Clement C. Moore, of whom mention has just been made, the illustrious Hamilton Fish, statesman, jurist, governor, Senator of the United States, Cabinet officer, diplomatist, commissioner in many international disputes, Churchman, representative in general and diocesan conventions, president of the Historical Society, and president-general of the New York Society of the Cincinnati, a bright and shining light in every position which he filled. To the list of your eminent parishioners may be added the names of Judge Henry E. Davies, also Henry B. Renwick for forty years an officer of the parish as vestryman, junior and senior warden.

The attention of one coming into this part of the town will be attracted by the sight of the old churchyard of St. Mark's, one of the most interesting of our urban cemeteries. Here some of the prominent families of the metropolis have their burial places, and here rest the mortal remains of many persons noted in the records of this city.

The first object to catch the eye is that great slab in the east wall of the church, which marks the entrance to the Stuyvesant vault. This famed and historic asylum of the departed is approached by a passage way cut through the foundation wall of the church, here five feet thick, whence a short corridor leads into the place, a room beneath the church, some forty feet in length. There are the remains of old Governor Stuyvesant, and near them is the dust of the English governor, Henry Sloughter, memorable for the part which he took in the suppression of the Leisler usurpation.

Outside, and close by, is the Minthorne vault,

in which Daniel D. Tompkins was buried, once Governor of New York, and Vice-President of the United States. Every writer of the annals of this parish has noted the interesting fact that these three men, Stuyvesant, Sloughter and Tompkins, representing the Dutch, English and American periods in the chief magistracy held by each in turn, here rest, close by one another, in the repose of the tomb. The walls of the church, and the grass-grown and shaded grounds about it murmur to the sympathetic ear with recollections of the past. Here, tablets, ancient and modern, and memorial windows invite the attention and implore the passing tribute of a kindly thought. Outside, rest together the bodies of the Rev. Drs. Harris and Anthon, the second and fourth rectors of the parish, as well as that of the Rev. William Berrian, my predecessor in the rectorship of Trinity Church; Col. Nicholas Fish, illustrious patriot, soldier and statesman; Peter Stuyvesant, the second foster father of the parish, as he might be appropriately styled; Peter and Elizabeth Schermerhorn; Philip Hone, the genial society leader, whose marble bust adorns the hall of one of our public libraries; Murray Hoffman, master in church and canon law; Ogden Hoffman, ornament of the New York bar; Mangle Minthorne, Abraham Schermerhorn, and Thomas Barclay, were buried here; and to theirs may be added the familiar names of Jacob Lorillard, Peter Goelet, Edward R. Jones, Mary Spingler, and so many more of the Schermerhorn, Winthrop, Goelet, Stuyvesant, Beeckman, and other old families of New York, that the time would be unduly prolonged in recording them. Of such are the silent assessors at the proceedings of this day, if indeed the spirits of the departed retain an interest in the places where once they dwelt in the frail tabernacle of the flesh.

This churchyard was used exclusively for vault interment; there were no open graves. In 1803 Mr. Peter Stuyvesant presented the parish with the plot of ground on Eleventh Street, between First and Second Avenues, which has been already mentioned, for a burial place. In 1851 a plot was purchased in the Cemetery of the Evergreens, to which the bodies were removed from the ground in Eleventh Street, so that now the parish has two burial places—this one at hand, known as St. Mark's Churchyard, and the more remote one, known as "St. Mark's Cemetery in the Evergreens." Peace be to the souls of all those who, here or there, sleep in Jesus Christ.

In concluding these obituary memoranda, an incident may be mentioned which will renew your interest in these proceedings.

We know that the tie between us who remain and those who are gone beyond is strengthened, and our communion one with another realized in the solemnity of the breaking of bread in the Lord's Supper. Now, it is a most interesting fact that the fair linen cloth which was used in Holy Communion, and covered the Lord's Table

ST. MARK'S CHURCH,

MAY 9TH, 1899.

THE NEW YORK
PUBLIC LIBRARY.

ASTOR, LENOX AND
TILDEN FOUNDATIONS.

at the consecration of this church one hundred years ago, has been reverently preserved, and presented to the church by our honoured and beloved friend, Dr. Stuyvesant F. Morris, and again covers the Holy Table at this centennial feast—a rare old piece of damask, with strange figures woven into the cloth, and indicating it as a fabric of some Dutch loom. Precious indeed is such a gift as this.

It is time to bring this brief sketch to a conclusion. Aware of its imperfections, I submit it to your kind hands as a contribution to that complete history of your ancient and interesting parish which will no doubt be written by some competent chronicler at a future day. In taking leave of you, the thoughts turn inevitably to the question, Who is now to take up and carry on this work? The parish, in this centennial year, is without a rector. The man on whom the mantle of his predecessors shall be cast; may he be all that you desire, the right man for this responsible position. With much interest do we look on meanwhile; nay, with some notions of our own about your coming rector; for it is in the line of human action to comment, occasionally, on the proceedings of our friends and neighbors, and even sometimes to proffer our advice, as the occasion may move us to that questionable liberty. Bear with me then if I suggest that what is needed here, at the beginning of this second century of your existence, is not one of those phenomenal, magnetic and electric individuals, joyfully described by the journalist as "abreast of the times," and "exponents of the best and most advanced thought of the day," not one of those orators to whom we listen with a depressing conviction that, whatever he may be saying, he is not preaching the old Gospel; whom the plainer sort can no more understand than the Northern farmer could understand his parson, while he drives forward on the line of discovery and through the drift of modern speculation about religion. The meteor which flashes through the darkness and for a brief moment or two illuminates the skies of night leaves thicker darkness behind it as it disappears. What you want is a man who comprehends the problem stated in old churches like this, churches which stand where they were first planted, witnesses for God and the Gospel, where everything else has changed.

I think that the highest honours to-day should be awarded to those parishes which cannot be forced or tempted to fly from their ancient seats; which are able to hold on, and hold their ground, without the help of pew rents, or the annual subsidies of rich persons who may change their minds, and must some day give up the ghost and pass away; which deem it a privilege and a duty to remain where lights are needed to lighten the darkness of the people, and accessible refuges for such as can be saved. Of such are my own old churches, away down in the lower parts of the city; of such are Grace Church, and St.

George's and others which might be named; churches becoming daily more distinctly churches for the people; mission churches in this enormous city, where missions and missionaries are needed as much as in the outlying heathen lands beyond. Endowments are needed for that purpose; to serve as buttresses and dykes against the angry flood; and well for those who are labouring, as more than one wise and prudent rector is to-day, for that end, and the safety of his sacred charge. A mission church let this be, and may he who shall take the spiritual headship be a man of that type of the servants of God; a preacher of the old evangelical, apostolic, Catholic religion; a man knowing how to commend to mind, heart, conscience, the message of redemption and salvation, in simplicity and sincerity; to wandering sheep, and erring folk, who throng our streets, and only need the friendly hand, the word in season, the touch of a father in God and a brother in Christ, to bring them back to their Father's House.

Brethren, peace be within your walls, and plenteousness within these courts; the plenteousness of Divine grace and light, the peace which comes to those whose souls are centred, not in man, nor in self, nor in an age which passes, and a knowledge which vanishes away, but in Him who is the same yesterday, to-day, and forever, to whom, one from eternity with the Father and the Holy Ghost, be ascribed all honour and glory henceforth and forever.

Brief Biographical Sketches of the Rectors.

REV. JOHN CALLAHAN.*

By his early and tragic death, this estimable young clergyman never, in fact, exercised the duties of the rectorship which he had accepted February 15th, 1800.

He was born in Charleston, South Carolina, in 1776 or 1777, and at the age of five years lost his father. Within a few years his mother married a Mr. Gibson, and, as several other children were added to the family, John's circumstances were very restricted. Dr. Robert Smith, Bishop of South Carolina, formerly rector of St. Philip's Church, Charleston, having observed the exemplary deportment and evident signs of promise in his young parishioner, adopted him as a son and gave him a liberal education, and, having prepared him for the ministry, admitted him to deacon's orders.

In the autumn of 1799 he accompanied his mother on a trip to the North for the benefit of

* On his tombstone in Charleston, and on the back of a miniature given by his mother to the family of Nich. Wm. Stuyvesant, Esq., the name appears as Callaghan.

Rev. John Callahan.

THE NEW YORK
PUBLIC LIBRARY.

ASTOR, LENOX AND
TILDEN FOUNDATIONS.

her health, and circumstances led to his officiating at St. Mark's. During the summer of 1798 the city was visited by a terrible epidemic of yellow fever, one in thirty of the population falling victims to it, and the inhabitants fled for their lives to the upper parts of the island. The disease reappeared in 1799, and, although not quite as severe as in the preceding year, many persons removed to Greenwich village and other safe localities. As St. Mark's was the only church near, a large congregation was drawn to it, and Mr. Callahan's services were highly acceptable, and in February, 1800, he received a unanimous call to the rectorship for a term of three years, "on condition that he conform to the rules, regulations and principles of the Protestant Episcopal Church as at present established." He accepted the call; but a desire to see his family and a wish to be advanced to the priesthood by his benefactor and spiritual father induced him to make the fatal visit.

On April 14, 1800, he was thrown from a carriage, and expired the same day, his last words being, "I am happy, for I die in the Lord Jesus." He rests near the middle of the western churchyard of St. Philip's Church, Charleston, beneath a monument inscribed as follows:

Jesus Wept.
Beneath this marble are interred the Remains of
The Reverend John Callaghan,
A native of this city, and late Rector of
St. Mark's Church
in the Bowery, New York,

who having, on April 14, 1800, received a mortal wound by a violent fall from a chaise, lingered a few hours in agonizing pain, and then, in perfect resignation to the will of Heaven, and in full reliance on the promises and hopes of the Religion he had ably preached and exemplarily practised, cheerfully obeyed the summons of his God and expired in peace.

He was in the twenty-fourth year of his age, and in the first of a happy, prosperous and honored Ministry.

HERE

Virtue and Religion, Learning and Patriotism, friendship and relative affection sustained a loss which it would be vain to attempt to estimate. Let the disconsolate Parents, the deeply affected Sisters and Brothers, the tears of his whole native city following his lifeless body to this receptacle of Mortality, attest how dearly he was loved, how reluctantly he was resigned.

BUT

Cease, ye afflicted surviving Relatives and friends of his departed Virtue, cease to repine at the Divine Decree; he is not dead but sleepeth, sleepeth in Jesus. Resigned then to your inestimable loss, rejoice in his unspeakable gain! Rest happy in the pleasing assurance that waited on by the same spirit that breathed Peace and Comfort to it in the last trying hour here his soul has winged its flight to the realms of Eternal Day.

On May 8th, 1800, intelligence from Bishop Smith of Mr. Callahan's death was laid before the vestry, and the following proceedings were had thereupon:

"The vestry, deeply afflicted with the melancholy event of the death of the Rev. John Callahan, and highly sensible of the great loss this Church has sustained in so excellent and valuable a pastor, and being desirous to pay every suitable tribute of respect to his memory,

"*Resolved:* That the church be hung in the usual mourning for three months, and that the churchwardens be directed to request the Rev.

Dr. Moore to deliver a sermon on the occasion in this church, on Sunday next (May 11, 1800);

"*And be it further resolved unanimously:* That to perpetuate the memory of his great virtues and excellencies, a marble monument be erected within the chancel of this church, on the west side of the altar, with such an inscription as the Right Rev. the Bishop of South Carolina may be pleased to devise.

"*Resolved:* That a committee of this vestry be appointed to acknowledge the receipt of the Right Rev. Bishop Smith's letters to Mr. Stuyvesant and Mr. Minthorne, and express the deep regret they feel for the loss that the Episcopal Church in general, and this church in particular, has experienced in the death of Mr. Callahan, and also communicate to him the resolutions this vestry has adopted in consequence thereof."

Bishop Smith replied as follows :

CHARLESTON, S. C., March 20, 1801.
VESTRY OF ST. MARK'S CHURCH.

Gentlemen : Long indisposition must plead excuse for my not answering your polite letter, received by Mr. Bowen. Indeed the request for an inscription for a monument to be erected to the memory of your late minister, the Rev. Mr. Callahan, is a difficult undertaking, considering the connection that had for years subsisted between us. Long a resident in my family, I had, from his amiable religious deportment and sweetness of manners, blended him into my family, and considered him as a son—and to write an epitaph on such a son was too trying for an old man. The pen,* to which few are equal, which wrote the pathetic discourse on your great loss (an extract from which I have read), would express your feelings on the mournful occasion much better than a wailing parent and friend, for as such I with pride rank myself; judging, however, of those feelings by my own, and that your wishes, avoiding all fulsome adulatory panegyric, are for an inscription marked with truth, I submit the following—of which some of the lines are a quotation, but greatly apposite—to your better judgment and shall not take it amiss if one from the more able pen of the eulogist who has appeared before you be made choice of.

I am, gentlemen, with respect and esteem,
Your affectionate, Humble Se'v't,
ROBERT SMITH.

The epitaph enclosed was adopted by the vestry without change, and placed upon the tablet, which was thereupon erected in the chancel recess. (See Appendix.)

REV. WILLIAM HARRIS, D.D.

William Harris was born at Springfield, Mass., April 29th, 1765. His mother was Sarah, a granddaughter of Wm. Pynchon, the founder of Springfield, and his father, named Daniel, was a deacon in the Congregational Church, in which his son, the subject of this sketch, received a li-

* Dr. Moore's.

cense to preach not long after his graduation from Harvard College in 1786, but the state of his health soon obliged him to abandon the exercise of the ministry, and he began the study of medicine under the direction of Dr. Holyoke, of Salem. Through reading Hooker's "Ecclesiastical Polity" he was led to become an Episcopalian, and upon the restoration of his health to enter the ministry of that Church.

In 1788 he had taken charge of the Academy in Marblehead, and he now accepted a call to the rectorship of St. Michael's Church, of that place, which was offered to him "provided he be Episcopally ordained." He was made a deacon on October 16th, 1791, in Trinity Church, New York, and advanced to the priesthood on the following Sunday in St. George's Chapel.

In the same year, 1791, on November 3d, he married Martha, the daughter of the Rev. Jonas Clark, of Lexington, Mass. They had seven children.

Mr. Harris continued to officiate both as teacher and preacher until 1801, when he received an unanimous call to St. Mark's to fill the vacancy caused by the death of the Rev. Mr. Callahan.

On February 2nd, 1802, he took his seat in the vestry, and was regularly inducted by the delivery and acceptance of the keys of the church. Soon after his settlement in New York, he established and conducted a classical school in the neighborhood of the rectory, which then stood east of Second Avenue on what is now Eleventh Street.

In 1811 Mr. Harris was elected president of Columbia College and received the degree of Doctor of Divinity from Harvard and Columbia. At the same time Dr. John M. Mason, the prominent Presbyterian divine, who had been proposed for the presidency, was made provost, an office created for him and carrying with it some of the administrative duties. This lightening of the president's work enabled Dr. Harris to retain the rectorship of St. Mark's, to the great satisfaction of his parishioners, until 1816, when, upon the resignation of Dr. Mason, the office of provost was discontinued, and the augmented duties of the presidency and failing health constrained Dr. Harris to resign his rectorship.

When he made the announcement to the vestry on November 14th, 1816, the following resolution was passed:

"*Resolved:* That the vestry deeply regret the necessity which will deprive them and the church of the services of their highly esteemed and much beloved rector, and that Mr. Minthorne, Mr. Lyde and Mr. Fish be a committee to express to him the grateful and affectionate acknowledgments of the vestry for his able, zealous and faithful performance of his parochial duties; of the high sense they entertain of his virtues, his piety, and exemplary deportment; of their unfeigned attachment, and fervent wish that his useful life may be long preserved in the enjoyment of health, happiness, and every temporal blessing, and that he may hereafter receive the reward of his labors in the service of his Redeemer."

The committee expressed the sentiments of the vestry in the following letter:

November 23rd, 1816.

THE REV. DR. HARRIS:

Reverend Sir: The information communicated by you to the vestry of St. Mark's Church of your intention to resign the pastoral charge of that congregation was received by them with unfeigned emotions of sorrow and regret; their feelings and sentiments on that painful occasion are recorded in the minutes of their proceedings, an extract from which is enclosed.

The duty of making this communication is assigned to us, and though painful the task of separating from our beloved pastor and friend, we derive some consolation from the reflection that our loss may result in his benefit, and that we shall not be totally deprived of the gratification of occasionally hearing his salutary and enlightened doctrines from that pulpit which he has for fifteen years so ably filled.

With sentiments of sincere friendship and regard, we have the honor to be, very affectionately, your obedient humble servants,

MANGLE MINTHORNE,
EDWARD LYDE,
NICHOLAS FISH.

Dr. Harris replied as follows:

NEW YORK, November 28th, 1816.
TO MANGLE MINTHORNE, EDWARD LYDE, AND NICHOLAS FISH, ESQRS.

Gentlemen: The perusal of your very affectionate letter, conveying a late resolution of the Vestry of St. Mark's Church, was a cordial to my heart. To be assured from you that my services were acceptable encourages me in the hope that my labors have not been altogether in vain. Happy for me, if it shall so be found, in that solemn hour when I shall be called to give an account of the manner in which I have discharged the duties of my late awfully responsible trust! If by occasionally preaching at St. Mark's I shall in any respect gratify the wishes of those whose happiness, both temporal and eternal, is so near my heart, what greater pleasure can I desire? My imperfect services, whenever you have need of them, are always at your command. I enclose a communication to the Vestry, and beg you will have the goodness to lay it before the Board at their next meeting. That you and your families may long enjoy the divine protection and favor, and that as members of the Vestry you may be directed to consult the true peace and prosperity of the Church is, gentlemen, the sincere prayer of

Your obliged, affectionate, and faithful friend,
WM. HARRIS.

In the enclosed communication to the vestry, Dr. Harris said: "Although I am sensible that your partiality and friendship have induced you greatly to overrate both my character and services, yet, as I doubt not your sincerity, I should be wanting both in gratitude and sensibility were I not to acknowledge that I entertain the highest sense of the value of the testimony you have been pleased to afford me, not indeed as an evidence of my desert, but of your sincere affection and friendship, than which (the divine favor and blessing excepted) nothing could be more grateful to my heart. Permit me, gentlemen, to observe, that I feel a satisfaction greater than I am able to express, when I consider that for fifteen years, between me and my vestry, not an unpleasant nor an unfriendly word has passed. In peace we have assembled, in peace we have consulted, and in peace we now part ; that the God of love and peace may continue to be with you, and that in the peace of Zion you may long rejoice, is the fervent prayer of your ever grateful, affectionate, and faithful friend."

On the preceding Sunday, November 24th, Dr. Harris had preached a very affectionate farewell sermon in St. Mark's, in the course of which he said : " Bear with me, I entreat you, while I briefly recapitulate a few of the most important truths, which, during my pastoral relation to you, I have inculcated from this sacred place. You are my witnesses, that I have not preached myself, nor sought my own glory, but Christ Jesus, and Him crucified. My chief object has been, as on the one hand, to humble the sinner, so, on the other, to exalt the Saviour. If my labors have not been altogether in vain, it is to be attributed, through the divine blessing, to the sincere desire which I have had to preach unto you, the pure and uncorrupted Word of God. I have never taught for doctrines the commandments of men, nor have I ever entered upon those intricate points in divinity, the discussion of which could contribute little to your edification. The fall of man, and his consequent depravity; his restoration by Jesus Christ; justification through faith in His atoning blood; the indispensable necessity of the renewing influences of the Holy Spirit to sanctify the heart; the awful punishment that awaits the impenitent, and the glorious recompense prepared for the righteous; and, finally, as the condition, though not the meritorious cause of salvation, a godly and a Christian life. These, my brethren, as you well know, have been the themes on which I have most frequently discoursed; and the duties and obligations resulting from these most important doctrines of the Gospel, to the extent of my ability, I have endeavored to enforce."

As a preacher, Dr. Harris was mild and winning in his manner. "His discourses," to quote his friend and parishioner, the Rev. Dr. John McVickar, "were plain, serious and persuasive; they came up to a celebrated critic's demand of what sermons should be—'the good sense of a good man'; and as delivered by him they had much of that power which flows from an earnest simplicity of expression ; they had the eloquence of sincerity, and went to the heart simply because they came from it."

In 1815 Dr. Harris preached the sermon at the funeral of Bishop Provost.

Upon his retirement from parochial work he devoted himself heart and soul to his duties as president of Columbia College, where he was greatly revered and beloved, "the students looking up to him as a father, and he, in turn, regarding them with an affectionate solicitude that was truly parental."*

In person he was of medium height, well proportioned. His complexion was pallid. In manner he was serene, kindly, grateful for the smallest favor, with an unpretending dignity, and although modest in the expression of his opinions, deliberately formed, he held them firmly, and displayed "that happy union of mildness and decision which intimidated the rebellious, while it disarmed them of all hostile feeling."

Dr. Harris died at Columbia College, on October 18th, 1829, passing away as in a gentle slumber. The funeral took place on October 20th, at 4 P.M., in Trinity Church, and was attended by representatives of the state and city government, all the learned societies, the alumni of the college and many others who walked in procession from the college to the church. Dr.

---

* Rev. Dr. J. M. Mathews, minister of the Dutch Church and trustee of Columbia College.

John McVickar preached the funeral sermon, and the interment was in one of the vaults in St. Mark's churchyard.

REV. WILLIAM CREIGHTON, D.D.

William Creighton was born in the city of New York, February 22nd, 1793. His ancestors on both sides were members of the Episcopal Church, William Bradford, the first printer in the city, being one of them.

Mr. Creighton was educated in Columbia College, and graduated in 1812, the second year of Dr. Harris's presidency. He was made a deacon by Bishop Hobart in the early part of 1815, and became assistant minister of Grace Church, New York. Some time before he had come under the favorable notice of the members of St. Mark's Church, during an illness of Dr. Harris, and the records show the following preamble and resolutions :

"WHEREAS, the congregation of St. Mark's Church have derived great benefit from the voluntary aid and assistance of Mr. William Creighton, since the indisposition of their respected rector, and the vestry conceiving it their duty, according to their means and ability, to remunerate any services rendered to the Church,

"*Therefore, resolved:* That the sum of $100 be appropriated for the purpose of purchasing some distinguished books on theology, and that the Rev. Dr. Harris be requested to procure such

THE NEW YORK
PUBLIC LIBRARY.

ASTOR, LENOX AND
TILDEN FOUNDATIONS.

works as he may judge most appropriate, to present them to Mr. Creighton, and request, in behalf of this vestry, his acceptance thereof."

Dr. Harris preached his valedictory on Sunday, November 24th, 1816, and on December 3rd Mr. Creighton accepted a call to the vacant rectorship, the duties of which he discharged faithfully until his resignation in 1836.

Dr. Creighton continued his usefulness in other stations so long after his separation from St. Mark's that his incumbency of nearly twenty years sinks into comparative obscurity, but it was really a period of growth for the parish, and, but for his domestic affliction, he would probably have long continued in a place where he was loved and esteemed.

Dr. Creighton's wife was Jane Schermerhorn, by whom he had three daughters, one of whom died in infancy. The others married the Rev. Dr. Edward N. Mead and Gen. George W. Morell. About 1823 Mrs. Creighton's mind became affected, and in consequence of this affliction the Doctor finally sought retirement in the country at what is now Scarborough-on-the-Hudson.

In 1830, Columbia College conferred the degree of Doctor of Divinity upon him, and on March 2d of that year he addressed a letter to the vestry informing them that in consequence of several returns of alarming illness he had been advised to try a sea voyage and change of climate, and asking for a leave of absence, which the vestry hastened to grant, expressing their regrets at the necessity, but voting him a year's leave with pay and a gratuity of $500 toward his expenses.

While Dr. Creighton was absent in Europe Bishop Hobart died, and, although no regular vestry meeting could be held, the members of the vestry met and passed appropriate resolutions.

During Dr. Creighton's rectorship the church building underwent several changes. An organ was purchased to take the place of those previously rented; the present steeple was built, as well as the Sunday-school building in the rear.

On May 5th, 1836, Dr. Creighton tendered his resignation in the following letter:

"Having decided to reside for the future out of the city, I herewith tender to you my resignation of the office which, as rector of St. Mark's Church for almost twenty years, I have had the honor to hold.

I am, gentlemen,
Very respectfully,
Your friend and servant,
WILLIAM CREIGHTON."

The vestry thereupon adopted the following resolution:

"*Resolved:* That the resignation by the Rev. William Creighton of the office of rector of the church of St. Mark's has been received by the vestry with those feelings which his connection with the congregation during a term of nearly twenty years is calculated to excite; that his irreproachable deportment as a man, and his sincerity in the discharge of the duties of his holy calling during the period of that connection will long be remembered and appreciated by his late parishioners; and that, on the occasion of this separation, he is accompanied by our wishes that he may enjoy every temporal blessing, and receive after this life the reward of eternal happiness.

"*Resolved:* That, as a memorial of the sentiments entertained toward the late rector, the sum of $500 be expended, under the direction of a committee of the vestry, in the purchase of books, to be suitably bound and inscribed, and to be presented to the late rector in the name of St. Mark's Church.

"*Resolved:* That the salary of the late rector be continued for six months from Easter last."

Dr. Creighton now removed to Beechwood, the residence which he had purchased on the banks of the Hudson, and the same year (1836) he became rector of Zion Church, Greenburgh (Dobbs Ferry), and also of Christ Church, Tarrytown, of which Washington Irving was for many years a member.

In 1845 Dr. Creighton resigned the rectorship of Zion Church, and the same year he was elected president of the diocesan convention, and re-elected every year until 1852, when Dr. Wainright was made Provisional Bishop.

These were the troubled years of Bishop Onderdonk's suspension, when party feeling ran very high, but a still stronger proof was given of the estimation in which Dr. Creighton was held by his election, in 1851, as Provisional Bishop. He declined the high honor from various considerations, chief among which was probably his domestic affliction. He performed the difficult duties of presiding officer with perfect fairness, ever courteous, and, when necessary, firm.

He was also chosen president of the House of Clerical and Lay Deputies of the General Conventions of 1853, 1856 and 1859.

In 1849 the church of St. Mary, at Beechwood, was founded by Dr. Creighton and his son-in-law, Dr. Mead, as a chapel-of-ease to Christ Church, Tarrytown, the ground and part of the cost being contributed by them. Dr. Creighton officiated at both church and chapel, without salary, until his death. On Sunday, December 4th, 1859, he preached a sermon upon the death of his friend and parishioner, Washington Irving. It is his only known sermon in print, and fairly representative of his style, and his eulogy of his friend might fairly be applied to himself. "What a beautiful example," said he, "does his life present for the imitation of us all! How does his humble though living faith in the Gospel scheme of redemption rebuke the pride of those who would be wise above what is written, and receive nought but what is perfectly plain and level to their finite comprehension! How does his conformity to the requirements of religion and of the Church of Christ, in the reception of the means of grace, contrast with the self conceit or the self-righteousness of those who 'care for none of these things,' and deem their own strength abundantly equal to the trials of life and to the 'working out of their own salvation!' How immeasurably superior is his active interest in all that can conduce to the welfare of the community to which he belonged, to that spirit of selfishness and unconcern which withholds aid and comfort from every plan which aims to improve the condition of those with whom we are joined in the bonds of Christian fellowship!"

During the last year of his life he was overtaken by a gradual paralysis, but continued to minister to his congregation, being brought into the church in a wheeled chair, until the disease affected his utterance, and he could only with an effort pronounce the benediction, and at last not even that.

He died April 23rd, 1865, and was buried under the chancel of St. Mary's church, a double tablet of white marble on a black background being placed in the church to his memory and that of his wife, who died the following year.

Dr. Creighton was of medium height and of courteous, dignified bearing. He was utterly averse to controversy and of a quiet, cheerful disposition. His utterances in public, such as his short addresses upon taking the chair in convention, were admirably expressed, and his sermons were calm, logical, and very clear.*

REV. HENRY ANTHON, D.D.

Henry Anthon was born in New York at No. 11 Broad Street on March 11th, 1795. At the age of fourteen he entered Columbia College, and graduated in 1813. He immediately began his preparation for the ministry, and was made a deacon on September 29th, 1816. Soon afterwards he became minister of the newly organized St. Paul's parish at Red Hook, on the Hudson, extending his labors to the adjacent villages. On May 27th, 1819, he was advanced to the priesthood by Bishop Hobart in the new church at Red Hook, which was consecrated the same day.

In 1819 he married Emilia Corré, of New York, and, his health having suffered from exposure in his missionary work at Red Hook, he spent the next two years in South Carolina. In 1821 he returned to New York and accepted the rectorship of Trinity Church, Utica. In 1829 he became rector of St. Stephen's, New York, and two years later an assistant minister in Trinity parish, officiating at St. John's Chapel.

In 1832 he received the degree of Doctor of Divinity from Columbia College, and in 1834 was elected secretary of the Board of Trustees of the General Theological Seminary, and also

* They have been compared to those of Bishop Ravenscroft, of North Carolina.

THE NEW YORK
PUBLIC LIBRARY.

ASTOR, LENOX AND
TILDEN FOUNDATIONS.

professor of Pastoral Theology and Pulpit Eloquence. In 1836, upon the resignation of Dr. Creighton, the vestry of St. Mark's extended a call to him, which he accepted in the following letter:

TO MESSRS. STUYVESANT AND LAWRENCE.

Gentlemen: The information of my election to the rectorship of St. Mark's Church in this city, which you did me the honor to communicate on Monday the 19th inst., and of my intention to accept that office were laid before the vestry of Trinity Church at their special meeting on the 23d, when the tender of my resignation as one of their assistant ministers was accepted. An offer was made by me in the same communication to continue my services in Trinity parish until the repairs and alterations at St. Mark's should be finished, and the vestry thereupon passed a resolution accepting the proposal "so long, until my place shall be supplied, as may suit my convenience." I purpose, therefore, in case the vestry of Trinity should not previously fill the vacancy, to continue in the discharge of duty in their parish until your church is ready, or nearly so, for service. Under these circumstances my rectorship, of course, is to date not from the time of my acceptance (I mean as it regards the salary), but from the time when my connection with Trinity parish actually ceases.

Allow me, gentlemen, to convey through you to the vestry of St. Mark's Church my thanks for the proof of confidence which this appointment manifests and for the very kind manner in which you have made their wishes known to me. Be pleased to accept my grateful acknowledgments.

With fervent prayer to God that He would send down upon me and the congregation committed to my charge the continual dew of His blessing for the honor of our Advocate and Mediator Jesus Christ,

I remain very respectfully your obedient servant,

HENRY ANTHON.
NEW YORK, December 27, 1836.

When the repairs were finished the church was reopened in May, 1837, and on the 11th of that month thirty-seven pews were sold for $11,-785, subject to annual rents varying according to location. The congregation then consisted of about 135 families.

Dr. Anthon, in his prime, with experience gained in various stations, threw himself ardently into the duties of his new position, and besides his proper parochial work, he was unwearied in his efforts to extend the Church into the remoter parts of the city and beyond. Needy parishes were assisted and missions established.

Dr. Anthon's opinions had been gradually undergoing a change; he had begun his ministerial career under the powerful influence of Bishop Hobart, and his associations were still with the party of which the Bishop had been the head, but he was gradually abandoning the exclusive ground upon which he had formerly stood, and his public protest against the ordination of Arthur Carey* severed him at once from his old associates. He was fiercely assailed in the press and elsewhere, but he went on his way undaunted and was cheered by the knowledge that those who knew him best approved of his action. The vestry of St. Mark's passed the following resolution on September 5th, 1843 :

"WHEREAS, since the last meeting of this vestry an extraordinary transaction has occurred in this diocese in relation to an ordination which was held in St. Stephen's Church, in this city, on the 2d day of July last, which has produced much public excitement and discussion, during which the course pursued by the rector of this church in relation to that matter has been the subject of extensive comment, and, in some instances, of severe animadversion; and,

*Arthur Carey, a young man of promise, was a candidate for the ministry, and applied to Dr. Hugh Smith, rector of St. Peter's, for the necessary certificate, but was refused, after several interviews, on the ground that he held views not conformable to the doctrines of the Protestant Episcopal Church. The Bishop (Onderdonk) examined him in the presence of eight leading presbyters of the Church, six of whom were satisfied with his explanations, but Drs. Smith and Anthon adhered to their belief that his sentiments were repugnant to the doctrines of the Protestant Episcopal Church, and when the Bishop made the formal appeal in the Ordination Service on July 2nd, 1843, in St. Stephen's Church, they rose and read their solemn protest and then left the church.
Arthur Carey died April 4th, 1844, in his twenty-second year, on his way to Havana for the benefit of his health, and was buried at sea.

"WHEREAS, the vestry of this Church, after a careful and deliberate review of the origin and progress of the controversy alluded to, are deeply impressed, as well with the purity of the motives by which the rector has been actuated, as by the prudence, firmness and wisdom which have marked his course, and have deemed this a fit and proper occasion to express their sentiments on this subject, therefore,

"*Resolved:* That the conduct of the rector in this trying emergency has met with the unqualified approbation of this vestry, and has given them a new guaranty that he will ever be found a vigilant sentinel to protect the church from all false doctrine, error and innovation."

To combat the opinions against which he had protested in the face of the whole Church, Dr. Anthon established a weekly paper called *The Protestant Churchman*, to which he contributed to the end of his life.

He was also one of the founders of the Protestant Episcopal Society for the Promotion of Evangelical Knowledge (1847); of the Pastoral Aid Society (1850) and of the American Church Missionary Society (1860).

In 1845 the vestry requested Dr. Anthon to deliver an historical discourse to commemorate the fiftieth anniversary of the laying of the corner-stone of the church, which he accordingly did, choosing for his text the words, "Hitherto hath the Lord helped us" (I. Sam. vii. 12). He said in part: "Of all the attributes which belong to God, is there one more striking than His immutability? While everything around us has impressed upon it the features of change and decay, He is yet 'the same, yesterday, and to-day and forever.' Year after year produces constant alteration in our neighborhood, in our families, in our situation and ourselves, but 'with Him is no variableness, neither shadow of turning.' Could anything teach a lesson to man, in his presumption and self-confidence, of the frailty and nothingness of his existence, it might be seen in the contrast between his own fleeting days and the duration of the natural objects placed along his path by their great Framer and Contriver. The broad river, not far from these walls, glides on, murmuring to the air and glistening in the sun, the same as it hath done in our youth, and in the youth of our fathers. The noble tree in the cemetery of the parish, which flourished in beauty in our childhood, flourishes in beauty and majesty to this hour. Even the works of human skill mock those that reared them. Where are the heads whose wise counsels designed, and the hands whose per-severing labors set up this sanctuary for a memorial unto God? Where are the beating hearts that so anxiously watched its progress, and so joyously hailed its completion? With an exception scattered here and there, they are stilled in the silence of the grave, to which the most of us shall certainly have gone down before another anniversary like this returns. The fruit of their earnest prayers and pious labors survives them in its strength, whilst they have crumbled into dust. Not so is it with the Almighty Architect, He whose eye was fixed upon the edifice when the corner-stone was laid, and who saw its headstone put on amidst the joyous acclamations of devoted hearts. He keeps to this day His oath and promise—' I am the Lord, I change not.' . . .

"'Hitherto hath the Lord helped us; our help is in the name of the Lord.'

"But there are those present this day who have never bowed themselves down before Him with this heartfelt acknowledgment. Why is it so? Ask of the days that are past; ask the question on this jubilee in our annals, the returning dawn of which it is certain shall lighten on many of our graves. Is not, my careless hearer, your heart beating and your blood flowing, and every faculty capable of enjoyment? Is not the Scripture proclaiming mercy in your ears, and does not the Holy Spirit proffer mercy to your soul? Whilst so sustained, and rich in outward blessings and privileges, where are *your* memorials? Are they in your hopes to be accounted righteous before God, centring by faith only, on the merits of Christ? Are they in your affections, clinging above all things unto Christ? Are they in your example, in all virtuous and godly living following after Christ? Sad, indescribably sad, is the reply which you are compelled to return; and yet, my brethren, notwithstanding your neglect and provocations, 'Hitherto,' at every point of your journey, have you received help from God. Shall it not be a motive, ere your sun goes down, to draw you under the influence of His Gospel, and to acknowledge the gracious authority of this mild and benignant Sovereign, that He may rule in your hearts without one rival of His throne ? Turn to Him without delay. Seek His face without reluctance, and He who has been a preserver of those interests which belong to time will prove, through the one Mediator and Advocate, an effectual helper to His presence in eternity."

During Dr. Anthon's rectorship many improvements were made in the church edifice, which assumed its present outward appearance a few years before his death.

On Christmas Day, 1860, Dr. Anthon, although ill and in pain, went through the full service, which included the administration of the Lord's Supper to 300 communicants. After eleven days of suffering, he died at noon on Saturday, January 5th, 1861. The funeral took place on January 8th, at 3:30 P M. The service was conducted by Bishop Horatio Potter, assisted by Drs. Tyng and Taylor and the Rev. Mr. Montgomery, and a great throng had gathered to render the last honors to him who lay there so calm and tranquil, with his official robe about him. He was laid at rest beside the church in which he had served so long.

On the same day the vestry of St. Mark's met and adopted the following resolutions:

"The vestry, feeling deeply the great loss that the Episcopal Church has sustained, and particularly this parish, in the death of Dr. Anthon, who has been their faithful pastor since December, 1836,

"*Resolved:* That the emblems of mourning in the church be continued until Easter, and that, in commemoration of the exalted virtues and character of Dr. Anthon, an appropriate monument be erected in the church, with a suitable inscription, expressive of his able and faithful services in the ministry.

"*Resolved:* That the vestry, sensible of the talent, zeal, and energy of their late rector, express their unfeigned sorrow at the loss they have sustained. His untiring devotion to the highest and best interests of the church in all its relations, and his unsparing, loving, and successful efforts at all times for the welfare of this parish, endear his memory to all who appreciate true piety and Christian example.

"*Resolved:* That this vestry respectfully offer to the widow and family of Dr. Anthon, and to the Rev. Edward Anthon, the assistant minister of this church, the expression of their heartfelt sympathy under this afflicting dispensation. And

"WHEREAS, one of the objects of our late rector, nearest and dearest to his heart, was church extension; and,

WHEREAS, the mission in Forty-Third Street, and the newly-erected church on Forty-eighth Street, are fruits of his successful efforts for the increase of the dispensation of Gospel truths;

"*Resolved:* That the new church be consecrated as the Anthon Memorial Church, in perpetuation of the fact that mainly through his influence and endeavors that church was erected by the Vestry of St. Mark's.

"*Resolved:* That a copy of these proceedings be sent to the widow of Dr. Anthon, and also to the Rev. Edward Anthon, the assistant minister.

"*Resolved:* That these proceedings be published in *The Protestant Churchman* and in other religious papers."

On January 12th the Episcopal clergy of the city met in St. Mark's Church and adopted resolutions upon the death of Dr. Anthon, and on Sunday, January 13th, the Rev. Dr. Stephen H. Tyng preached his funeral sermon.

In person Dr. Anthon was small, with dark hair and eyes; in his later years his hair turned snowy white. He was of a nervous temperament; tenacious of his principles; energetic in carrying them out, and unflinching in the performance of his duty. Although frequently engaged in heated controversy, he remained gentle and courteous, cheerful and affectionate, and "his life was," in the words of the tablet erected by the vestry, "an example of singular purity and consistency."

REV. ALEX. H. VINTON, D.D.

Alexander Hamilton Vinton was born in Providence, R. I., May 2nd, 1807, and was the second youngest of the five sons of David and Mary Atwell Vinton. He received his academic education at Brown University, and after graduating studied medicine at Yale College, receiving the degree of M.D. in 1828. He settled in Pomfret, Conn., where he remained three years, and then abandoned his medical practice, entered the General Theological Seminary, and immediately upon his graduation, in the spring of 1835, was made a deacon by Bishop Griswold. He took temporary charge of Grace Church, New York, in the absence of the Rev. Dr. Taylor, and in October was called to St. Paul's Church, Portland, Me., where he only remained about six months, and became rector of Grace Church, Providence. In 1842 he went to St. Paul's Church, Boston, Mass. Here he remained sixteen years, going thence to the Church of the Holy Trinity, Philadelphia, Pa., in 1858. It was of this work that Phillips Brooks, who had grown to manhood under his pastoral care in Boston, said: "The whole ministry of Dr. Vinton in Philadelphia is one of the brightest and sunniest pictures which the annals of clerical life have anywhere to show. It is like a summer's day and moves in life and music. The powers were all tested. The position was assured. The range of a pastor's duties

THE NEW YORK
PUBLIC LIBRARY.

ASTOR, LENOX AND
TILDEN FOUNDATIONS.

had been measured in the fields in which he had already worked. There was neither the anxiety of the young minister afraid of the indefiniteness of his work, nor the discouragement of the old minister who feels already the premonitions of decay."

Upon the death of Dr. Anthon, in 1861, the vestry of St. Mark's offered the vacant rectorship to Dr. Vinton, and after careful consideration he accepted it and began his duties in May. The conditions here were quite different from those in Philadelphia; there the Church was new, with no old traditions; here the parish was already more than half a century old. And his vocation, to quote Dr. Rylance, " was pre-eminently that of a Christian preacher ; being the best rhetorician, probably, that the Protestant Episcopal Church has produced throughout its entire history." He recognized the need of a different kind of work in the great district eastward of the church, and before long a mission was started on Avenue A, which prospered so well that in 1866 the Bishop in his annual address could say that there were " such numbers that the chapel would not hold them." It was becoming evident, however, that to meet the new conditions of the neighborhood caused by the influx of foreigners in larger and larger numbers, the character of the work of St. Mark's would have to be changed, and Dr. Vinton, with his threescore years, fully realized the difficulty of the task for a man of his age and he must, moreover, have felt his great, but special gifts could be used to better advantage in a different field.

On October 15th, 1869, he laid the following communication before the vestry:

"I have received an invitation to the rectorship of Emmanuel Church, Boston, which, after much consideration, it has seemed proper for me to accept.

" I beg leave, therefore, to tender to you my resignation of the rectorship of St. Mark's Church, which I would wish to take effect at the close of November. Acknowledging the many kindnesses that have been extended to me by the vestry, with the assurance of my regard to the members personally,

I am, gentlemen,
Very respectfully and truly,
Your friend and servant,
ALEX. H. VINTON."

The resignation thus tendered was accepted, with a suitable expression of acknowledgment of his labors and services during his ministry in St. Mark's Church.

He had formed the resolution of retiring from active parochial work upon reaching the age of seventy years, and in the autumn of 1877 he accordingly resigned the rectorship of Emmanuel Church, and retired to the old homested at Pomfret, where he employed his time in study and rural pursuits, continuing, however, to lecture every winter before the Cambridge Divinity School.

In 1881 he went to Philadelphia to take part in the consecration of the new Church of the Holy Trinity (his former parish), preaching the sermon on Thursday, April 21st. On Saturday morning, the 23d, he became ill, and the disease, which proved to be pneumonia, grew so rapidly worse that it terminated fatally on Tuesday morning, April 26th. The funeral service was held at the Church of the Holy Trinity on Thursday afternoon, April 28th, and was conducted by the Bishop of the diocese, assisted by the Bishop of Delaware, the Rev. Drs. Phillips Brooks, C. M. Butler and C. D. Cooper, and the Rev. W. N. McVickar, the rector of the parish. The interment took place on Friday morning, the 29th, in Swan Point Cemetery, Providence, R. I., where his grave is marked by a stone inscribed as follows:

Alexander Hamilton Vinton,
son of
David and Mary Atwell Vinton.
Born in Providence
May 2, 1807.
Died in Philadelphia
April 26, 1881.

On the west side:
" Faithful unto death."
On the east side:
" I will give thee
a crown of life."

In person Dr. Vinton was a large man, of commanding presence, with greyish-blue eyes, brown hair, and a rather pallid complexion. He spent but a few of his more than three-score and ten years in St. Mark's, but a mural brass, placed on the western wall of the church by a few friends after his death, testifies to the esteem and affection in which he was held; and one who knew him well, indeed, Phillips Brooks, testifies that "He was a splendid man to succeed in the charge of a parish. Many a good and saintly old minister half grudges the work which yet he prays that his successor may have the grace to do in the parish where he himself can work no longer. But I am not the only minister here to-day who could tell you of the quick and earnest sympathy and the ever-ready encouragement and pleasure with which this great predecessor in our parishes made us rejoice whenever he came among us and looked with kindly interest to see how well our younger hands were doing his old work."

Besides occasional sermons, Dr. Vinton published a volume of sermons in 1855 and his course of Bohlen lectures.

"In the great circle of Christ's doctrine," he said in a sermon to the graduating class of the Cambridge Divinity School, "of which the cross with its redemptive idea is the luminous and single centre, there are various segments of practical, spiritual development into which that central redemptive idea naturally opens itself.

The different forms and modes of religious life and thought lie all along the periphery of the circle; yet each one of them is a natural outcropping of the central element—salvation by grace and atoning blood. These several forms of religious truth and practice are adapted to the various temperaments of men, and to the varying spirit of the times in which they live. The practical, the contemplative, the æsthetic temperaments shall each find its congenial and satisfying truth, as a part of the great Christian circle of truths. But either of these presented exclusively, and without its clear and announced connection with the central truth of the cross, would lose its sacred worth, and utterly cease to be of the truth as it is in Jesus.

"For example, while sacraments and orderly worship, while philanthropy and self-sacrifice for others, while the lofty contemplation of God and His grand moralities and eternities are clearly part of a true Christian life, and grow out of the radical idea of a suffering and redeeming God, yet either of them may be separated from its vital connection with that root, and become no better than a gospel that man has made. A Platonist might teach the same doctrines of contemplative piety, and be a pagan still. A moralist might practise all the philanthropy, exalting the beauty of Jesus' life all the while, but worse than ignoring His sacrificial death; and the sacramentalism and the ritualism might all be done by a Hebrew or a

Hindoo, the one not knowing Christ at all, the other hating Him. The ritualism, the philanthropy, the contemplativeness, would all be forms of religious development, representations of ideas and truths found in the great circle of Christian truth, not 'the truth as it is in Jesus,' because dislocated from the great redemptive idea, which is their only vitalizing power.

"While, then, we yield, as we legitimately may, to the contemplative spirit of the age, which rejoices in a high-toned, spiritual hymnody, depicting the sublimest devotional reach of the soul; while we cannot resist, but must answer and meet, that practical spirit which exacts the Christian's labors and gifts in all the forms of philanthropic effort; and while, too, we gratify the æsthetic demands of the times, in making God's house and worship as beautiful as befits their holiness; yet, oh! let us never forget that all these are not live truths, unless Christ be in them as the dying Redeemer, who bore our sins and their penalty in His own person; and that none of these religious deeds are done as they should be done, unless they come from the grateful remembrance of His cross."

The influence of Dr. Vinton was not confined to the parishes where he ministered, but was felt by the Church at large. "In the debates of the General Convention he was recognized as a master, and he never addressed that body without commanding the attention of all who heard him. He always had the courage of his opin-

THE NEW YORK
PUBLIC LIBRARY.

ASTOR, LENOX AND
TILDEN FOUNDATIONS.

ions, and he struck many a stalwart blow in defence of the school of thought of which he was a recognized leader and head—the Low Church party. He was a foeman worthy of any man's steel, and he compelled those who differed with him most widely to respect the force of his logic, and the truth and honesty of his convictions."*

REV. JOSEPH HINE RYLANCE, D.D.

Dr. Rylance, the first *rector-emeritus* of St. Mark's Church, held the office of rector for a longer period than any of his predecessors.

Although they were all men of eminence, few remain who knew them, and it seemed proper to record some particulars of their lives and characters to preserve them a little longer from that oblivion which rapidly swallows up the memory of even the eminent of a past generation.

But Dr. Rylance, we hope, may long be able to tell his own interesting life story, and to exemplify in the pulpit the high order of sacred eloquence of which he is master.

He was born in the City of Manchester, England, on June 16th, 1826. In 1861 he graduated from King's College, London, with honors, being made an A.K.C. In the same year he was admitted to the order of deacons by the Lord Bishop of Winchester, at Farnham Palace. In 1862 he was advanced to the priesthood. On

* *Churchman*, May 7th, 1881.

that occasion the Rt. Rev. C. P. McIlvaine, D.D., Bishop of Ohio, preached the sermon.

Dr. Rylance's first and only curacy was at St. Paul's Church, Westminster Bridge Road, London.

Bishop McIlvaine, who was a close friend of Bishop Sumner, urgently invited Dr. Rylance to come to America, and in 1863 he transferred his "orders" to the Diocese of Ohio.

He had taken a keen interest in our Civil War, and when his intention to come to America became known to those with whom he had been acting in vindicating the Government of the United States in its efforts to suppress the rebellion, he was deputed, with the Rev. Dr. Massey, of London, to present an address signed by many thousands of sympathizers with the "North" in England and France to President Lincoln. This they did in July, 1863; shortly after the battle of Gettysburg.

In September, 1863, Dr. Rylance became rector of St. Paul's Church, Cleveland, O., and while in this position received the degree of D.D. from the Western Reserve University.

In 1867, after repeated invitations, he accepted the rectorship of St. James's Church, Chicago, Ill. He was also made Dean of Northern Illinois.

At Easter, 1871, he became rector of St. Mark's, and was at once recognized as one of the leading preachers of the city. Social questions in the light of the Christian religion have always engaged his earnest attention, and among his published writings are "Social Questions," 1880, and "Pulpit Talks on Topics of the Time," 1882 ; and to these he added a book, "Christian Rationalism," in 1898.

On November 18th, 1898, he laid the following communication before the vestry :

TO THE WARDENS AND VESTRYMEN OF ST. MARK'S PARISH IN THE BOWERIE.

Gentlemen : I hereby resign my rectorship of St. Mark's Church in the Bowerie, to take effect, if you shall so will, on the first of December, '98.

I cannot trust my feelings at this time to say more than to acknowledge, which I do very gratefully, your uniform brotherly kindness toward me, and your forbearance toward my manifold infirmities.

Let me " improve " the occasion, however, as preachers used to say—a very solemn occasion to me—to commend to your increased watchfulness and co-operation the many interests of St. Mark's Church. For more will depend upon you, under the blessing of God, in the consolidation and expansion of its work, than upon any ability you may find in the man who may succeed to my place.

J. H. RYLANCE.

The vestry, in accepting the resignation, adopted the following resolution :

"The Rev. Joseph H. Rylance, D.D., rector of this parish during twenty-seven years, having at this vestry meeting, November 18, 1898, tendered to us his formal resignation in pursuance of an intimation given us some time ago, that he had arrived at a time of life when he felt the need of being relieved from the care of a parish, We, the wardens and vestrymen of St. Mark's Church in the Bowery, in accepting his resignation, which we do with profound regret, desire to place upon the parish records our appreciation of his long and faithful service, in which he has worthily upheld the traditions of his distinguished predecessors.

"Called to this parish in 1871 as its fifth rector in the century of its existence—the Rev. William Harris, subsequently president of Columbia College, having served from 1800 to 1816, the Rev. William Creighton from 1816 to 1836, the Rev. Dr. Henry Anthon from 1836 to 1861, and the Rev. Dr. Alex. Vinton from 1861 to 1869—he has, by his ripe scholarship, his liberal theology, his unstinted devotion, made an imperishable place in the hearts of his people.

"In a time of trial, such as comes to few, he evinced the fortitude of a man and the piety of a Christian. Never did he swerve or falter, and out of the fires of a terrible experience he came victorious, with malice toward none, with charity for all.

"We only bid him adieu as our rector, and we hope he may long be spared for wise counsel and loving intercourse.

"As a testimonial of our appreciation we tender him the position of *rector-emeritus.*"

On December 1st Dr. Rylance's incumbency, the longest in the history of the parish, came to an end. On the 10th he sailed for Italy, having upon the intervening Sunday once more occupied his pulpit, at the special request of the vestry. He spent the winter in Rome, and was still abroad at the time of the church's centennial.

An Historical Sketch of St. Mark's Church.

PREPARED BY THE CLERK OF THE VESTRY.

St. Mark's Church in the Bowery stands upon ground consecrated to the service of religion nearly two hundred and fifty years ago, and never since used for any secular purpose; for although there was an interval between the disuse of the old Dutch Chapel and the erection of the present edifice, yet the presence of the dead preserved the hallowed character of the spot, and amid all the changes that have swept over this city, it remains the oldest church site on the island of Manhattan.*

Very soon after his arrival as Director-General of the New Netherlands, Peter Stuyvesant began acquiring land far up in the woods above the little city lying behind its palisades along the line of the present Wall Street, and upon this estate he built a country residence, about the exact location of which there is some doubt, but whether the mansion stood on Tenth Street, just beyond the grounds of the church, or on Twelfth Street, east of Third Avenue, the sit-

---

* The first place on the island where stated religious services were held was the loft of Francis Molemaecker's horse-mill, built 1626, on the north side of what is now South William Street, between Broad and William Streets.

The first *church* was erected in 1633 on the shore of the East River (Pearl Street), between Broad and Whitehall Streets. This was used until 1642.

uation of the chapel which he built some time before 1660 is certain.

The church of St. Nicholas had been erected within the walls of the fort below the present Bowling Green, at a time when the hostility of the surrounding Indians was a very grave danger, and thither the people resorted from near and far, for under the judicious administration of the last of the Dutch governors the farms began to spread outward again. New Haarlem was firmly established, and a little settlement sprang up around the governor's farm, or "Bouwerie." For the accommodation of these people, as well as his own household, and particularly the negro slaves, of whom some forty lived in the neighborhood, the governor built a little chapel where, in the year 1660, regular clerical ministrations were begun by Domine Henry Selyns, a poet in Dutch and Latin, the friend and correspondent of Cotton Mather.

Before this time it is probable that the schoolmaster read the Scriptures and the Creed to the people, but in the year named the village of Breuckelen (Brooklyn), then containing 134 inhabitants, having called Domine Selyns, found itself unable to raise his modest salary of less than $500, and applied to the Director-General for assistance. He agreed to contribute 250 florins ($100) a year on condition that Domine Selyns should preach at the Bouwerie on Sunday evenings. So the arrangement was made and continued for four years, until the clergyman's return to Holland. His successor was Samuel Megapolensis, a doctor of medicine as well as theology.

It is difficult to realize the remoteness and almost inaccessibility of the little settlement in those early days, but some idea of it may be obtained from the fact that in this very year, 1660, one Jansen petitioned to be relieved of his tenancy of some land near the "governor's Bouwerie, as he had to go two miles through a thick wood," and his fears were not unreasonable, for five years before the savages had desolated all the outlying districts.*

The road to the farm left the city gate at the present corner of Broadway and Wall Street, and followed the line of Broadway, Park Row and the Bowery to Harlem and so on to Albany and Boston. It early became known as the road to the governor's Bouwerie, and in time the Bouwerie road was shortened to the Bowery, a name which still survives, while all around has changed.

No record remains of the architectual appearance or the size of Stuyvesant's chapel, but it probably faced what is now Stuyvesant Street, which was originally a road running through the

---

* Another amusing instance occurs in the old records where the City Fathers on June 15th, 1665, resolve that " Focke Jans, living at the Bowery, is allowed to lay in every week half a barrel of strong beer free of excise, in consideration of the great expense which he has to incur before he can get the beer to his house, inasmuch as he has to convey it in his own wagon with his own men, also the leakage of the beer on the road."

And so late as the year 1683 a bounty was offered for wolves killed on the island between the city and Harlem.

farm, and the vault yet in existence determines its location.*

After the capture of New Amsterdam by the English in 1664, Governor Stuyvesant went to Holland to render an account of his administration and then returned to his Bouwerie, where he continued to reside until his death in 1672. He was buried in the vault under the chapel, whither he was followed, in 1687, by his widow, who by will † left the chapel to the Dutch Re-

* In a paper read before the New York Historical Society, Mr. Benjamin Robert Winthrop, a descendant of one of the first wardens of St. Mark's, said: "From the construction of this vault and the position of the entrance, I have come to the conclusion that the western gable of the old church must have stood about ten or twelve feet from the eastern gable of the present edifice. My reason for this conclusion is that what appears to have been an entrance has been closed up by brick work, while the rest of the vault is of solid masonry."

† Extract from the will of Judith Stuyvesant : I doe further bequeath to my said Cousen Nicholas Bayard and to his wife and Child or Children (if desired) a bureing place In the Tomb or Vaught of my Last deceased husband In the Chappell or Church att my Bowry ; And In case it should happen that my sayd Church or Chappell did Come to decay or for an other Reason be demolished I doe hereby declare and publish it to bee my Last will and Testament that of the materialls and Rubbage, of sayd Chappell bee made a buildeing Sufficient ffor a Coover upon the said Vaught. . . . And I doe by these presents further by forme of a Legasie Give and grante to the Reformed nether dutch Church or Congregation of the Citty of New Yorke My Testracies Church or Chappell Seituated On my bowry or farmes Together with all the Revenues proffitts and Immunityes As aloso with all the Incumbrances to the said Chappell belongeing Or appertaininge To have and to hold the said Chappell and appurtenance after the time of My decease Unto the Overseers of the said Congregacon to the use aforesayd for Ever with further power iff they see cause to demolish or displace the same and to Employ the Materialls thereof to such Uses as they shall think ffitt & expedient Provided that in such ·case of the sayd materialls bee made and built all and whatsoever In the Inclosed Testament Is Exprest and Required for the preservation of the tombe or vaught which was built by my deceased husband in the said Church.

formed Church of New York, to dispose of as they saw fit, provided the vault was preserved.

It appears, however, that either the Consistory of the Dutch Church found it inexpedient to continue services in the chapel or the bequest proved unavailable for the reason that the testatrix had only a life interest in the property, and the building soon fell into a state of dilapidation, until little remained except the foundation.

In the meantime the Stuyvesants had joined the English Church, Nicholas William, a great grandson of the governor, being a vestryman of Trinity Church from 1760 to 1773, and his brother Petrus from 1793 to 1799.

Nicholas William died unmarried in 1780, and thus Petrus became the representative of the family and heir to the broad ancestral estate.

With the return of prosperity after the close of the Revolution the population of New York increased rapidly, and the frequent occurrence of the yellow fever—1791, 1793, 1795, 1798 and 1799—drove large numbers into the salubrious localities northward of the city, where many of them found permanent homes. The churches slowly followed, but until St. Mark's was built, the only Episcopal churches were Trinity and St. Paul's Chapel at their present locations, St. George's Chapel in Beekman Street, and Christ Church in Ann Street.

In 1793, Petrus Stuyvesant, actuated no doubt by the same motives as his great grandfather more than a century before, proposed to the vestry of Trinity Church the erection of a church upon his land, toward which he offered to give £800 ($2,000) and a plot of ground 150 by 190 feet, or twelve city lots.

This generous offer was taken into consideration on July 8th, 1793, and it was resolved to accept it and to "take measures for building a church accordingly as soon as the situation of the corporation will admit thereof, and that Messrs. Stuyvesant, Gaine and Jones be a committee to enquire what aids can be obtained from well disposed persons toward the same."

Mr. Stuyvesant declined to serve on the committee, and Mr. Van Horne was appointed in his place, but it does not appear that they succeeded in raising any funds, for two years elapsed, and then, January 19th, 1795, the vestry of Trinity resolved to "raise the sum of £5,000 ($12,500) for building a church on the land of Peter Stuyvesant, Esq., in conformity with his proposals," and Messrs. Carmer, Gaine, Van Horne and Stuyvesant were appointed a building committee.

On St. Mark's Day, Saturday, April 25th, 1795, the corner-stone of the new church was laid by Bishop Provoost.

The work progressed very slowly, a delay having occurred, apparently in 1798, for in that year the building committee was authorized to contract with C. Halstead for carpenter's work, and with Messrs. Pers and McComb for mason's work. The committee had been previously instructed to proceed with the work until the church was under cover and no further.

On Thursday, May 9th, 1799, it was reported finished, and was consecrated the same day by Bishop Provoost, with a sermon by the Rev. Dr. Benjamin Moore, and the administration of the Holy Communion.

Although the body of the church has remained intact to the present day, the appearance of St. Mark's in 1799 was very different from what it is now, for there was neither steeple, porch nor fence, and the stone walls had not yet been covered with plaster. Inside, the pews in the gallery were unfinished, there was no organ, and much painting remained to be done, for which Trinity paid a bill of 72£ 15s. 9d. What colors were used is not stated in the records, but there are grounds* for surmising that the walls were lemon, the ceilings and pews white. The light streamed freely in through the plain glazed windows, and on the short winter afternoons candles furnished the illumination when the daylight faded away.

The building actually stood, as its name implies, on a farm—in the midst of green fields and trees. The built up portion of the city was still far away. Maps of the period do not even indicate any streets on the East side above Houston, then known as North Street, and in fact no

* The reason for thinking that the popular colonial colors were used is that some thirty years later, when the first considerable improvements were made, several of the painters name those colors in their estimates, which were probably based on existing conditions.

ST. MARK'S CHURCH IN 1799.

THE NEW YORK
PUBLIC LIBRARY.

ASTOR, LENOX AND
TILDEN FOUNDATIONS

city plan had yet been adopted for the region above that line, while below only straggling houses approached it. The upper part of the island was generally in its original state of hill, forest and morass, with farmhouses and country residences scattered along the Albany post road and at the most picturesque points on the East River.*

As St. Mark's was nearing completion, the question arose whether it would not be better to organize it as a separate parish, instead of retaining it as a chapel like St. George's and St. Paul's. As Trinity, by the charter of May 6th, 1697, which subsequent legislation did not materially change, had been made the "sole and only parish church" in the city of New York, the proposal to erect another parish raised legal questions which were referred to Messrs. Richard Harison and Alexander Hamilton, and their opinion being satisfactory, measures were accordingly taken to make St. Mark's a separate church.

Mr. Harison, who was a member of Trinity vestry, reported that the first step necessary would be to convey the church and land to trustees in trust for the corporation of St. Mark's Church when the same should be formed, and on August 19th, 1799, the following gentlemen were appointed trustees : Peter Stuyvesant, Francis

* The neighborhood of the church then presented the conditions now prevailing some thirty miles up the Hudson. It was a charming rural region where people went to spend the summer. As late as 1807 Dr. Harris reported to the Diocesan Convention that the number of communicants was 60 to 70 in winter; 120 to 200 in summer. Besides the Stuyvesant farm, there were several large estates, so that the regular congregation consisted of a few rich families and their servants and dependents.

Bayard Winthrop, Gilbert Colden Willett, Mangle Minthorne, Martin Hoffman, Wm. A. Hardenbrook and George Rapelje.

Mr. Rapelje declined to act, but the others met in the church on August 27th and organized by electing Mr. Stuyvesant, president, and Mr. Hoffman, clerk, and it was resolved to take collections in the church every Sunday to defray the incidental expenses.

On September 24th, the trustees met again and adopted the following resolution:

"WHEREAS, it is necessary, in order to carry into effect the complete organization of this church, that an election for two churchwardens and eight vestrymen should immediately take place; and it being more proper that they should be chosen by the persons composing the congregation of the church than appointed by the trustees, and in order to interest the congregation for this purpose,

"*Resolved:* That the pews in the lower part of the church be sold at public auction on Wednesday next, at eleven o'clock in the morning, on a lease of five years, at the highest rent that can be obtained, payable half yearly; and that notice be given in the public newspapers* in the

---

* On September 26th and 27th the notice appeared in the *Commercial Advertiser* as follows, with the correction of an obvious typographical error:

PUBLIC AUCTION.

On Wednesday next, the 2d October, at eleven o'clock, will be sold at Public Sale at St. Mark's Church in the Bowery

THE PEWS

on a lease of five years, payable semi-annually.

city of New York, and at every public place about the Bowery."

According to the notice, the trustees met in the church on October 2d, and reserving pews Nos. 9, 41, 76 and 108, they sold thirty-seven pews at annual rents ranging from 30 to 140 shillings New York currency, the total amounting to 96£ 16s. 0d., or $242.

Pew No. 9 was presented to Mr. Stuyvesant rent free for five years, in recognition of his liberality to the church; Nos. 41 and 76 were set apart for the use of the rector, churchwardens and vestrymen, and No. 108 was reserved for " the Governor and other respectable characters who may occasionally attend divine service in the church."

The numbers of the pews have been changed a little since that day, so that what is now pew No. 102 represents the old Governor's pew, occupying relatively the same place on the west side of the church as the Stuyvesant pew does on the east, and until 1835 each of these pews was surmounted by a canopy, as the President's and the Governor's pews are to this day in old St. Paul's.

All the pews taken were near the front in the middle and both side aisles and none under the gallery were taken. The one which brought the highest price (140 shillings) was the old No. 82 on the west aisle, which was leased by Wm. Thomas, whose son Alfred, born August 23d, 1799, was the first child baptized in St. Mark's Church, September 1st, 1799.

In the middle aisle, to the left, sat Lieut.-Col. Nicholas Fish in pew No. 71, and opposite, in pew No. 46, Gen. Horatio Gates. Behind Gen. Gates sat Francis Bayard Winthrop, and two pews further back John Slidell, whose son of the same name is better known through the Trent affair.

The names of most of the first members of St. Mark's appear on the pages of "The Old Merchants of New York," and many of them were related by intermarriage. It was a well-to-do, almost aristocratic congregation, but the picture would be incomplete if we failed to take note of the dusky faces in the background, for in nearly all the wealthier families there were still negro slaves, and one of the stipulations in the grant of a burial ground, made by Petrus Stuyvesant, in 1803, was that "the rector, churchwardens and vestry, their successors and assigns, shall at any time hereafter permit and suffer the interment of any person who now is and has been the slave of the said Petrus Stuyvesant, and the children of all such persons, in the said burial ground, without the charge of any mortuaries, burial fee, or other ecclesiastical duties whatsoever."

At the conclusion of the sale, rents were affixed to the remaining pews at which Mr. Hoffman, the clerk, was requested to rent them, and at a meeting of the trustees, held October 8th, he reported the sale of six more pews for a total of 13£ 4s., or $33.12½.

It was now resolved that on Friday, October 18th, St. Luke's Day, the adult male members of the congregation should meet to incorporate themselves and elect wardens and vestrymen, and notice to this effect having been given in the church on the two preceding Sundays, according to the law of the State (Act, March 17th, 1795), the election was duly held immediately after Morning Prayer.

Mr. Petrus Stuyvesant was chosen chairman, and Messrs. Anthony L. Bleecker and Andrew Hamersley tellers.

The following gentlemen were elected:

WARDENS.

Petrus Stuyvesant, Francis B. Winthrop.

VESTRYMEN.

Gilbert C. Willett, Wm. Ogden,
Martin Hoffman, George Turnbull,
Wm. A. Hardenbrook, Nicholas W. Stuyvesant,
Mangle Minthorne, James Cummings.

Easter Tuesday was fixed upon as the day for future annual elections, and it was determined that the legal title of the corporation should be the Rector, Churchwardens and Vestry of the Protestant Episcopal Church of St. Mark's in the Bowery in the City of New York.

The certificate of incorporation * was filed in

* Mr. P. G. Stuyvesant prepared the certificate of incorporation and other necessary papers, and the amounts of the fees for drawing, engrossing, etc., are interesting:
Drawing certificate of incorporation and acknowledgment.. $3 50
Engrossing certificate of incorporation and acknowledgment. 1 50

the county clerk's office November 22d, 1799, and the church property was subsequently conveyed by the trustees to the corporation.

The first meeting of the vestry was held on November 5th, 1799, with Mr. Winthrop in the chair.

Peter Gerard Stuyvesant, a son of Petrus Stuyvesant, was elected clerk to the vestry, and Mr. Hoffman, treasurer. James Jarvis was appointed clerk to the church, and Luke Kip, sexton. The office of clerk was kept up for many years afterward, being generally held by the tenor singer in the choir. It was his duty to lead the congregation in making the responses.

It was resolved that the salaries of the clerk and the sexton be the same as those allowed at St. Paul's, namely, $100 per annum for clerk and $75 for sexton.

It was also resolved to ask Trinity for further financial aid, as the burden of supporting the new parish bore very heavily on a few, nor did Trinity fail to respond, for when the petition from St. Mark's was received, the committee on leases was instructed to designate such lots, estimated to produce an annual revenue of £200, as it might be proper to convey to St. Mark's, and, as we shall see, the gift was ultimately more than doubled.

Town Clerk's fee for recording...	$ 75
Drawing and engrossing release from trustees to corporation of St. Mark's...	6 00
Engrossing release from corporation of St. Mark's to corporation of Trinity...	3 00
Engrossing two releases from Trinity to St. Mark's...	16 00

On December 17th, the vestry met again, and Mr. Hoffman resigned the office of treasurer and Mr. Hardenbrook was elected in his stead. The clerk was directed to provide a seal and a book for a " record of births," *i.e.*, a baptismal register.

The first pew committee was appointed, consisting of Messrs. Minthorne and N. W. Stuyvesant.

Steps were now taken to secure a rector, Messrs. Willett, Hardenbrook and Ogden being appointed a committee to wait on the Rev. John Callahan to learn informally if he would consider a call. Having received a favorable reply, after he had communicated with his spiritual father, the Bishop of South Carolina, the offer of the rectorship was made and accepted early in February, 1800. Undoubtedly out of deference to the wishes of Mr. Callahan, the engagement was made for three years only, and, as was not infrequent in the early days of the Protestant Episcopal Church in the United States, the condition* was annexed that "he conform to the rules, regulations, and principles of the Protestant Episcopal Church as at present established."

Mr. Callahan wished once more to visit his relations and also to be made a Priest by Bishop Smith, so it was agreed that the rectorship should begin at Easter (April 13th), and as a gratuitous allowance for services rendered prior

* The same phraseology was used in the call of the Rev. Mr. Creighton, and when the Rev. Mr. Harris was called to St. Michael's Church, Marblehead, Mass., in 1788, it was on the condition that " he be episcopally ordained."

to that date, the vestry, on March 4th, resolved to make him a present of $300 immediately.

The meeting at which this action was taken was mainly occupied in considering financial difficulties. A report was presented showing that the sum of $697.87 was due for expenses incurred since the establishment of the church, and that $650 would be needed for current expenses during the coming year. In addition, $1,250 would have to be raised for the rector's salary. The income from pew rents was less than $300 and the total collections for a year not over $150. These sums, with the $500 which the promised grant from Trinity would produce would still leave an annual deficit, so it was proposed to open a subscription to raise $1,250 a year for three years to pay the rector's salary, and it was resolved to dispose of the pews which had been reserved for the governor, rector and vestry.

It seems that during Mr. Callahan's absence the Rev. Seth Hart* was engaged as minister, for on May 8th a vote of thanks to him was passed and also a resolution to allow him $7 a day for his services.

At the same meeting the sad intelligence of Mr. Callahan's death was laid before the vestry and appropriate resolutions passed, as described more fully in the sketch of his life.

On May 14th the committee on repairs was authorized to have a fence erected on the boun-

---

* Mr. Hart came from Connecticut and succeeded John Henry Hobart at Hempstead, L. I., where he remained many years.

daries of the property of the church, which till then had stood in the open fields.

Pending the transfer of the lots with which Trinity intended to endow her struggling offspring, the amount of the rents derived from them was paid to St. Mark's.

On August 27th a committee was appointed to offer the rectorship to the Rev. John Henry Hobart,* in deacon's orders, at St. George's Church, Hempstead, L. I., but he declined it to accept the position of assistant minister in Trinity Parish.

The vestry's next choice was the Rev. Philander Chase,† rector of Christ Church, Poughkeepsie, but he also declined, in deference to the advice of his vestry.

On the last day of the eighteenth century another attempt was made to fill the vacancy, it being resolved to apply to the Rev. Cave Jones, then connected with St. George's Parish, Accomack, Va., but he, like Mr. Hobart, had also been invited to Trinity Parish, and, like him, accepted.

It would appear that the vestry was getting discouraged by these repeated failures, for ten months elapsed before they made another attempt. In the meantime, however, the services

---

* John Henry Hobart was born 1775; deacon, 1798; priest, 1801; assistant minister of Trinity Parish, 1800; Bishop-Coadjutor of New York, 1811; Bishop, 1816; died, 1830.

† Philander Chase was born 1775; deacon, 1798; priest, 1799; rector of Christ Church, Poughkeepsie, 1800; Christ Church, New Orleans, 1805; Christ Church, Hartford, 1811; missionary in the West, 1817; Bishop of Ohio, 1819; Bishop of Illinois, 1835; died, 1852.

were kept up, the Rev. Frederick Beasley having been engaged to read divine service at a salary of $750 a year. Mr. Beasley was at the time a deacon ministering in St. John's Church, Elizabethtown, N. J. He afterward held various rectorships and became provost of the University of Pennsylvania (1813-1828) and Doctor in Divinity. He died in 1845.

On October 16th, 1801, it was resolved to call the Rev. Theodore Dehon,* rector of Trinity Church, Newport, R. I., but he also, "not without some reluctance," declined, for although his "temporal interests" would have been "greatly promoted by an acceptance," he could not bear to separate from those whose "endearing attention to his ministry" had bound them to him.

Although still unable to get a rector, the financial prospects of the church were improving, for on November 28th, 1801, in response to the repeated requests for assistance, the vestry of Trinity gave notice of the selection of thirty lots on the church farm† which they

---

* Theodore Dehon was born in 1776; deacon, 1797; priest, 1800; rector of Trinity Church, Newport, R. I., 1797; St. Michael's Church, Charleston, S. C., 1810; Bishop of South Carolina, 1812; died, 1817.

† The Dutch West India Company reserved a tract known as the Company's Farm, which lay between Fulton and Warren Streets and Broadway and the North River. When New York became English this farm was known successively as the Duke's, the King's, the Queen's. In 1670 it had been enlarged by the purchase of what was called the Domine's Farm and Old Jan's Land. These tracts were, for the most part, narrower than the original farm, but they extended as far north as Charlton Street. In 1705 the whole estate was granted to Trinity Church by Queen Anne, and then became known as the Church Farm.

would transfer to St. Mark's upon the receipt of a release and quitclaim, as advised by legal counsel. The condition was, of course, agreed to by the vestry of St. Mark's, and in due time a deed for the lots was received. They were located as follows: Warren Street, five lots; Provoost (now Franklin) Street, six lots; Church Street, one lot; Reade Street, nine lots; Harrison Street, three lots; North Moore Street, six lots.

On December 23d, 1801, the rectorship was offered to the Rev. Wm. Harris, of St. Michael's Church, Marblehead, Mass., and accepted by him, and on February 6th, 1802, he took his seat in the vestry and was canonically inducted by the delivery and acceptance of the keys of the church in the presence of Peter Gerard Stuyvesant and Asa L. French, the sexton.

The anxiety about the settlement of a rector being now happily dispelled by the acceptance of Dr. Harris, and the financial embarrassment relieved by the liberality of Trinity, measures were adopted for building a parsonage. Subscriptions were asked for the cost of the building, while the land was given by Mr. Petrus Stuyvesant—a plot 56x95 feet, lying on the south side of Stuyvesant Street, east of Second Avenue, or what is now Eleventh Street.

By December 6th, 1802, the sum of $1,900 had been subscribed, but this was not enough for the purpose, so it was resolved to ask Trinity for a loan of $800 to complete the rectory.

Failing in this, the required amount was borrowed from Mr. Minthorne, a member of the vestry, and the house was finished and occupied by Dr. Harris, with his family. A well and pump were provided near by.

On August 26th, 1803, Mr. Stuyvesant made another munificent donation of land to the church for a cemetery—a plot 242 x 190 feet opposite the rectory lots, and extending eastward. In the following spring it was resolved to fence in the burial ground with "neat palings in front and boards in their original state on the sides and rear."

In July, 1804, for the second time in its then brief history, the church was draped in mourning, for, on the twelfth of that month, Alexander Hamilton had breathed his last, and on the twentieth, the vestry resolved, out of respect for his memory, to keep the church in mourning six weeks.

At the same meeting, in recognition of his numerous benefactions to the church, the vestry resolved "that pew No. 9, now occupied by Mr. Stuyvesant, be appropriated and reserved by this corporation for the use of himself and family, forever, free of any charge of rent whatever." Pew No. 1 was reserved for the rector.

In the meantime, some improvements had been made in the church, the pews in the gallery having been finished, and the first piece of plate for the Communion service—a silver flagon—had been purchased. In 1805, the service was completed through the generosity of Messrs. Ten Eyck and Hardenbrook, who gave $83.34 and $20, respectively. The first of the memorial tablets, Mr. Callahan's, had also been erected.

On August 18th, 1804, the second sale of pews took place, and the growth of the church is shown by the fact that fifty-seven pews were sold on a seven years' lease, subject to a rent of $562.50, as against thirty-six pews and $242 five years before.

Among the new pew-holders the honored name of Renwick now first appears (pew 73), also R. Lenox (pew 78), and Bishop Moore (pew 116).

In 1805, the vestry were troubled about the construction of the section of the Act of the Legislature requiring religious corporations to make triennial reports, between the first of January and the first of April, of all their property, real and personal, under pain of dissolution. They had failed to do so within the specified time, and upon taking legal advice as to the proper course to pursue, it was deemed expedient to take steps for a reincorporation under the Act of March 27th, 1801.

Due notice thereof having been given in the church, a meeting for reincorporation was held on July 23d, and the following gentlemen were elected:

WARDENS.

William Ogden,   Mangle Minthorne.

Vestrymen.

George Turnbull,	Martin Hoffman,
Thomas Ten Eyck,	Nich. W. Stuyvesant,
Nicholas Fish,	Anthony Norroway,
Harry Peters,	Wm. A. Hardenbrook.

On October 7th, Petrus Stuyvesant, who had aided so liberally in the establishment of the church, died, in his seventy-eighth year, and was laid at rest in the family vault under the church.

In 1806, the movement began for the erection of a steeple—that architectural feature which adds dignity and character to a church.

The subject frequently occupied the attention of the vestry during 1806 and 1807. Estimates were obtained of the cost of building a steeple or cupola, and aid was asked from Trinity for this object, which was not fully realized until twenty years after.

While Trinity could not do all that was asked, the sum of $500 was granted, and also the small bell of St. Paul's. This was hung in the low tower, with which the vestry were forced to content themselves. The little bell continued to ring out over the fields until they were swallowed up by houses and the struggling country church had become a wealthy city parish. In 1837, a new bell (the one still in use) having been provided, an application was received from St. Clement's Church for the loan of the old bell, which was granted for ten years, and then the gift was made permanent. The old bell continued thirty-eight years longer in service, until 1875, after which it was heard no more.

In 1807, the first vaults were built in the grounds adjoining the church, the vestry having resolved, on February 11th of that year, "that any member of this church have permission to make a vault for the interment of the dead in either of the two cemeteries, on paying to the treasurer of this corporation for every foot front by eight feet in depth in the clear the sum of $2.50."

In the early days every church in the city had its burial ground, and some of the busiest spots down town once afforded resting places for the quiet dead. In Wall Street, opposite New, stood the Presbyterian church, surrounded by graves; in Garden Street (Exchange Place), between William and Broad Streets, the old Dutch church, and on the corner of Nassau and Pine Streets, the French church, and many more which have long since disappeared; so that to-day St. Mark's remains one of the few city churches which still preserve their adjacent cemeteries.

The administration of Dr. Harris went quietly on, his own placid temper shedding its influence over the life of the parish, and making the period one of peaceful, prosperous growth. No startling events mark the annals of the time, and it is pleasing to note that the friendly relations with Trinity were kept up, and a glimpse is afforded of that happy time before the hurry and rush of the present. Thus in 1809 Dr. Harris asked for a leave of absence for about a month to visit friends in Boston, and he informed the vestry that he had made arrangements with the clergy of Trinity to supply the pulpit during his absence. Some years before the name of John Henry Hobart, of Trinity Parish, appears on the records as a sponsor for one of Dr. Harris's children.

In 1810 the rector of St. Mark's had the honor of preaching the sermon before the Diocesan Convention, which met in Trinity Church on October 2d. He spoke of the character of a Christian minister from the text I. Thess. ii. 10–12.

During the same year (1810) several organ builders asked permission to put up an organ in St. Mark's Church, presumably because in those days the factories were not provided with suitable rooms for testing the quality of a large organ, and probably also in the hope of selling the instrument when it was once in place.

The vestry gave the required permission to Mr. Erben and early next year steps were taken for the purchase of an organ; in the meantime one was rented for $70 a year.

In 1811, the seven-year pew leases expired, and instead of holding an auction sale, as on the two former occasions, the vestry resolved, "That the pew-holders after the expiration of their present leases have the privilege of renewing the same for the term of seven years, subject to the payment of the same purchase money and annual rent as heretofore, and that the pew committee be authorized to dispose of any pews which may be surrendered in like manner as if retained by the present holders."

Since the establishment of St. Mark's six more Episcopal churches had been organized in the city, namely St. Stephen's (1805), St. Michael's (1807), Grace (1808), St. James's (1810), Zion (1811), and during the same year St. George's Chapel was made an independent parish. The members of some of these churches claimed the right of voting at the elections in Trinity because until 1814 its legal title ran "the rector and inhabitants of the city of New York, in communion of the Protestant Episcopal Church in the State of New York."

As every one of these churches had been assisted more or less by Trinity, this attempt to interfere in the Trinity elections did not seem right to the vestry of St. Mark's, and they expressed their sentiments in the following letter, a copy of which the clerk was directed to transmit to the vestry of Trinity Church under the seal of the corporation of St. Mark's:

TO THE VESTRY OF TRINITY CHURCH.

NEW YORK, April 16th, 1812.

Gentlemen: We believe that it is eminently the duty of Christians to live together in brotherly affection; and that the obligations to discharge this duty lie, with greater weight, on the members of the same Church. Feeling, as we ought, the full force of this sentiment, we have heard with regret that some of our Episcopal brethren assert the claim of a general right in all of the Episcopal Churches on this island to vote, at your elections, for churchwardens and vestrymen. Whatever color may be given to this claim by any ambiguous words to be found in your charter, we sincerely take pleasure in declaring that the congregation of St. Mark's Church, which we represent, have no desire to assert the claim, and that we will, at any time hereafter, cheerfully unite with your respectable body in an application to the Legislature if the measure shall be thought expedient for an act to explain the charter, and confine the right of voting solely to the congregations of the churches under your immediate government. And we beg leave to add that we shall cheerfully unite in such application, as well from the earnest wish we have to restore harmony and establish peace by removing the uneasiness which we understand the claim has created in the minds of many of the members of Trinity Church, as from the strong sense we entertain that the measure itself is dictated by the natural fitness of things, and more especially by the never to be forgotten rule of doing to others what, under similar circumstances, we should like to be done to ourselves.

With the most respectful consideration,
We are, gentlemen,
Your humble servants.

In 1811 Dr. Harris accepted the presidency of Columbia College, and in 1816, owing to the augmented duties of that office, he resigned the rectorship of St. Mark's Church.

"For fifteen years," says Dr. Anthon, "the period in which his flock had the benefit of his ministrations, he went in and out among them, revered as a father, esteemed very highly in love for his work's sake, showing in his life and conversation that uncorruptness, gravity, sincerity, and sound speech, which, whilst it marked his character with so many essential elements of true excellence, secured to him the unshaken confidence and warm affections of his people."

They offered him a pleasing token of their regard some time after his resignation by voting to set apart a pew for his use.

Upon the resignation of Dr. Harris, the vestry lost no time in calling the Rev. Wm. Creighton, already favorably known to the congregation of St. Mark's through his ministrations two years before during the illness of Dr. Harris.

Dr. Creighton began his rectorship at Advent, 1816; and during the twenty years that he filled the office great changes were taking place in the city and in the church. A plan of streets for the whole island had been adopted in 1811, and although some of them have not been opened to this day, most of those in the neighborhood of the church were laid out during his rectorship. St. Mark's no longer was a suburban church—

an outpost of church extension—and even before 1816 the first period of struggle had ended and the congregation had acquired stability, so that it was deemed inexpedient to resort to frequent auction sales of pews, and as early as 1811 the pew-holders were allowed to continue their leases for seven years longer at the rates then in force, and in 1818 it was resolved "that the practice of selling the pews of this church for a term of years to the highest bidder be discontinued from and after the expiration of the present leases, and instead thereof that the pew rent be raised $33\frac{1}{3}$ per cent., to commence with the new leases on the first day of October next. Also, resolved that the present pew-holders have the privilege of renewing their leases for the term of seven years from that day, subject to the payment of the annual rent herein established."

In 1821 the question of purchasing an organ came up again, one owned by the Rev. Mr. Wainwright* and others having been offered for $800. A committee was appointed to make the purchase, but concluded that the price was too high, and so reported. Mr. Erben now offered to loan one on condition that his son be appointed organist. To this the vestry agreed, and the arrangement continued until 1823, when a contract was made with Thomas Hall for an organ having one set of keys, nine stops, and

---

* Jonathan M. Wainwright, born 1792, assistant minister of Trinity, 1819; rector of Grace, New York, 1821; Trinity, Boston, 1834; St. John's Chapel, New York, 1836; Provisional Bishop of New York, 1852; died, 1854.

688 pipes. The cost was to be $1,150, and the vestry were so well pleased "with the faithful manner in which the work was done" that they gave Mr. Hall $50 more than his contract price. Two years later a swell and the bass part of a choir organ were added.

In 1822, plans for completing the steeple with either a spire or a cupola had been again under consideration, and although they were not carried out for some years, in the meantime it was resolved to prepare a room in the belfry to be used as a vestry room; it would appear that the meetings up to this time had been held in the church itself.

On November 12th, 1824, the rector laid before the vestry a communication from the Standing Committee of the General Theological Seminary of the Protestant Episcopal Church, addressed to the Episcopalians of New York, soliciting contributions toward the erection of permanent buildings on the land given by Clement C. Moore,* a vestryman of St. Mark's Church. It was therefore resolved "that this vestry feel a deep interest in the success of the measures above mentioned, in reference as well to the general prosperity of the Theological

---

* At a meeting of the committee of the General Convention, on the subject of the Theological School, held in Philadelphia, February 7th, 1819, "a letter was laid before the committee by Bishop Hobart, from C. C. Moore, Esq., of the City of New York, addressed to him, containing an offer of the grant of sixty city lots, provided the buildings of the Theological School should be erected thereon." The offer was accepted. Appendix to the Journal of the General Convention 1820.

Seminary, as to its permanent establishment in the city, and that the rector, Col. Fish, Messrs. Ortley, Lee, Murray and Lyde, be a committee on the part of this church to obtain contributions from the members thereof, toward the erection of the said edifice."

During the next two years the sum of $1,352 was collected from members of St. Mark's.

In 1825 oil lamps were substituted for the candles, which had been the means of lighting the church up to that time, and green Venetian blinds were placed on the east side of the church.

In 1826 the first mention of a Sunday-school appears. One hundred and twenty scholars were enrolled, and Hamilton Fish was one of the early treasurers of the Sunday-school Association.

On December 7th, 1826, the plans of Thomson & Town for a steeple of brick or stone were accepted, the cost not to exceed $5,000. The work was delayed for some time on account of the uncertainty about Stuyvesant Street, which was not on the commissioners' plan, and was liable to be closed and built upon. This would have made it necessary to change the entrance to the church to Eleventh Street, and objections were raised to the erection of the steeple at what would then be the rear of the church. It was finally decided that, as the foundation at the south end had been prepared to support a steeple, it should be placed there. The Common Council had been petitioned to make Stuyvesant Road a public street, but the request had not been granted; and Gideon Lee (afterwards mayor), at that time a member of St. Mark's vestry and an alderman, advised his associates in the vestry to repeat the application in the following year, as it was probable that the composition of the Common Council would be changed by that time and a more favorable response might be looked for. And so it turned out. The steeple was built, and the street was established up to Second Avenue. The pew rents were increased 50 per cent. at this time for the purpose of gradually reducing the debt which had been created by the erection of the steeple. The pew rents now (1828) amounted to $943 a year.

At this period and for some years after, the neighborhood of the church was broken up by the extension of the different streets eastward of Second Avenue. In 1828 the rector was authorized to let the parsonage and to receive the rent for his own use. He took up his residence at No. 23 St. Mark's Place.

The opening of Twelfth Street in 1829 and of Eleventh Street afterwards cut off corners of the cemetery and made a readjustment of the boundaries necessary, which was done by exchanges with the adjoining proprietors, an Act of the Legislature passed February 4th, 1814, permitting such exchanges, with the consent of the chancellor.

In 1830 Dr. Creighton obtained leave of absence for a year, as he had been advised to try a sea voyage and change of climate for the restoration of his health. The vestry voted to continue his salary, and gave him a present of $500 toward his expenses. The Rev. John M. Guion* was appointed the rector's substitute during his absence, at an annual salary of $500, and the ordinary routine business was transacted by a committee to whom certain powers had been delegated before the rector's departure, as it was believed that no valid meeting of the vestry could be held during the rector's absence from the country. For the same reason no election of wardens and vestrymen was held in 1831.

During Dr. Creighton's absence, on September 12th, 1830, occurred the death of Bishop Hobart, and the members of St. Mark's vestry met, on September 17th, at the home of one of the wardens, and adopted the following resolutions:

"It having pleased Almighty God, in His wise providence, to remove from this world the Right Rev. John Henry Hobart, D.D., Bishop of the Protestant Episcopal Church in the diocese of New York, this board, deeply sensible of the pre-eminent zeal, talents and attainments

---

* John Marshall Guion was born in New York City, in 1801; deacon, 1829; priest, 1830, and minister-in-charge at St. Mark's; Saybrook, Meriden, New Britain, Conn., 1832–53; St. Paul's, Baltimore, 1853; chaplain of Auburn Prison, 1854; Trinity Church, Seneca Falls, 1855; S.T.D. Columbia, 1865; died, 1878.

of their deceased diocesan, in order to express their unfeigned grief at the loss they have sustained, in common with the Church throughout the state, in being deprived of the superintending care of their venerable head, but at the same time humbly submitting to Divine Providence;

"*Resolve:* That St. Mark's Church in the Bowery be hung in the usual mourning until the festival of Christmas. That, in further testimony of our respect for the memory of our late Bishop, we will attend his funeral and wear the usual badge of mourning thirty days. That a copy of the foregoing resolutions be handed to the relict and family of our late Bishop, and that they be published."

On June 20th, 1833, the church lost a valuable member, Col. Nicholas Fish, who had been vestryman from 1805 to 1821, and warden from that year until his death. On September 26th, the vestry met and adopted appropriate resolutions.

St. Mark's Church had now stood for thirty odd years. It had a large congregation, and counted among its members men of prominence in social and political life. The down-town streets, which had been filled with substantial residences, were rapidly yielding to the inroads of business and their inhabitants were forced to seek homes uptown. St. Mark's Place promised at one time to become one of the most fashionable residential streets. Second Avenue, Lafayette Place and Broadway were favorite localities.

Up to this time, with the exception of the steeple, only slight alterations and repairs had been made about the church, but now extensive changes were planned. To accommodate the growing congregation, the advisability of extending the edifice at the chancel end was considered. This plan was rejected, however, and instead a two-story building, containing rooms for the Sunday-school and vestry, was erected in the rear of the church at a cost of about $2,500. This was finished in 1835. Next year a vane was placed upon the steeple, and a subscription for a clock was opened.

On May 5th, 1836, Dr. Creighton tendered his resignation, which was regretfully accepted. On May 31st the vestry ordered that the mortuary fees* should in the future be paid into the treasury, and that the perquisites for interments heretofore paid to the rector be discontinued.

In October,† 1836, the building committee was empowered to close the church for the purpose of making the contemplated alterations, which were completed in the following spring. The

---

* The burial fees at this time were as follows: For members of the congregation over twelve years of age $8, public vault, $10; under twelve years of age, $4, public vault, $5. For persons not members of the congregation the charge was double.

† During the time since Dr. Creighton's resignation, the Rev. Henry Tullidge and several others had been engaged to officiate. Mr. Tullidge (afterwards D.D.) was born in Portsmouth, England, 1812; came to America with his parents about 1824 and settled in Albany, N. Y.; his principal clerical charges were, Galena, Ill., Erie, Pa., Pequea, Pa., Bloomsburg, Pa., Swedesboro, N. J., Prof. of Systematic Divinity in Gambier, O., Norwalk, O., Aspinwall, Panama, San José, Costa Rica, Pequea, Pa. Died in Philadelphia, 1897.

interior was painted, and instead of only putting mahogany tops on the old pews, as had been proposed, new ones were put in ; a fine pulpit was erected at the back of the chancel, which was extended in front, and a new baptismal font was provided. Gas was introduced. A stone portico was added, as there was no longer any doubt about Stuyvesant Street and the approach to the church.

The new pulpit was of the type jocosely called "three-deckers." Originally, the Communion table stood in the chancel in the same place as at present, but was hidden from view by the pulpit and reading desk. The new arrangement was designed to give prominence to the table by placing the high pulpit with the reading desk below at the back of the chancel and the Communion table in front of it. The new pulpit was of white enamelled wood, and was greatly admired for its elegant proportions ; it remained in use until the time of Dr. Vinton. The useless furniture, lamps, etc., of the old pulpit and most of the pews were presented to Calvary Church,*

* WHEREAS, by the voluntary contributions of such of the friends of our Heavenly Father who have at heart the extension of His Kingdom upon earth, and by the kindness and liberality of the wardens and vestrymen of St. Mark's Church in this city, in presenting the necessary pews and trimmings, the wardens and vestrymen of Calvary Church have been the humble instruments, in the hands of God, of so far effecting their object in erecting a place of public worship in that destitute part of our city, on the Fourth Avenue near Thirtieth Street, as that the same has by His blessing been consecrated to His service and for which they desire to and do hereby make their humble acknowledgments to Almighty God that He hath thus far prospered them; and

then located "near Fourth Avenue and the Harlem road" (Fourth Avenue near Thirtieth Street). The remaining pews were given to the Church of the Nativity, at Williamsburgh, L. I., and the old font to Zion's Church, Wappinger's Creek (Falls).

In the meantime, on December 17th, 1836, Dr. Anthon had accepted the rectorship, and the church was reopened by him May 7th, 1837.

In 1835 Peter Gerard Stuyvesant founded the St. Mark's Church in the Bowery Professorship of Ecclesiastical History* in the General Theological Seminary, upon which the trustees reported in part as follows : " The General Convention and the Church at large will hear with lively satisfaction of another evidence of Christian munificence, and will recognize in it with

---

WHEREAS, they are left to some considerable extent in arrears, to meet which they must still depend upon the bounty of their Christian friends;

Therefore, the said wardens and vestrymen of Calvary Church, in view of their past success, and assured that, in dependence upon the divine blessing, their efforts cannot fail to procure for them such additional aid as may be required,

Resolved : To persevere until their whole task of entirely discharging their debt shall be fully accomplished.

Resolved : That the foregoing preamble and resolution, signed by the clerk of the vestry, be published in *The Churchman*, and a copy of the same be sent to the wardens and vestrymen of St. Mark's Church.

N. B. MOUNTFORD,
Clerk, etc.

* The following gentlemen have occupied the chair: The Rev. Wm. Whittingham, S.T.D., LL.D. (afterward Bishop of Maryland), 1836-40; the Rev. John D. Ogilby, D.D., 1841-51; the Rev. Milo Mahan, D.D., 1851-64; the Rev. George F. Seymour, D.D., LL.D. (now Bishop of Springfield), 1865-78; the Rev. Thomas L. Richey, D.D.

thankful hearts the good providence of God in promoting the welfare of the Seminary. At a meeting of the trustees a few days since in New York, an offer was communicated to them on the part of Mr. Peter G. Stuyvesant, of that city, to found a Professorship in the General Theological Seminary, the department to be designated hereafter by the founder, and the Professorship to be named after St. Mark's Church in the Bowery. For founding the same Mr. Stuyvesant offered to give the sum of $25,000, upon condition that such steps were taken by the trustees as would secure to the founder of a Professorship the right to nominate to the trustees within one month after the endowment some person as Professor; should such nomination not be approved, the founder then to have a right to make a second nomination of some other individual; and should such second nomination be also rejected, the trustees then to have the power to nominate to and fill the Professorship themselves. This very generous proposition was unanimously adopted by the trustees, and a resolution passed tendering their cordial thanks to the donor, and appointing a committee to confer with him 'for the purpose of carrying into effect his enlarged, pious and benevolent views in relation to the proposed Professorship.'" The first nominee, the Rev. Dr. Hawks, declined. Mr. Stuyvesant then named the Rev. Wm. R. Whittingham, whose nomination was approved in 1836.

Upon reopening the church in 1837 a new policy was adopted in regard to the pews. The extensive improvements had cost a large sum of money and the church was running heavily into debt. When the alterations were under consideration a loan not to exceed $10,000 had been authorized, but before all the work was done the expense amounted to $16,000. In order to raise ready money for the reduction of the debt, it was decided to *sell* the pews upon a *permanent* lease, subject to a fixed annual rent according to location. An auction sale was accordingly held on Thursday, May 11th, 1837, at which twenty-seven pews were sold for a total of $11,785. The prices ranged from $100 to $705, with one in the gallery at $50, and the rents from $10 to $30 and $5 in the gallery. Soon afterward four additional pews were disposed of at private sale on the same terms as those sold at auction. The amount obtained was $1,950. The old names of Stuyvesant, Winthrop, Fish, Morris, etc., appear among the purchasers, but there are also many new ones. (See appendix.)

In 1838, Dr. Anthon began a Parish Infant School, the vestry agreeing to allow the use of a room, fuel, etc., while the salary of the teacher and other expenses were raised by subscription. This school was maintained for about sixty years, until it was no longer needed on account of the ample accommodations in the public schools near by.

On April 18th, 1838, another public sale of

pews took place, at which twenty pews were sold for $7,275.

The opening of Second Avenue left an irregular plot of ground between the boundary of St. Mark's churchyard and the avenue. Peter Gerard Stuyvesant, the owner of the land, offered to sell it to the corporation of St. Mark's Church, and also to construct vaults thereon, for which he was to be repaid when the vaults were sold. The vestry accepted the offer, and on May 28th, 1838, the transfer was made. The land acquired began at the northwest corner of Second Avenue and ran west 12 feet 3 inches ; thence along the line of the churchyard for 131 feet to Eleventh Street ; thence east 79 feet 4 inches and back to the starting point 105 feet 1 inch. The price paid for this tract was $10,000, and it afforded room for forty-three vaults.

On June 2d, 1838, the building committee was directed to procure plans and estimates for an iron railing around the churchyard to replace the picket fence which had been put up in the year 1800, and which was now in a dilapidated condition. This led to the erection of the present railing at a cost of about $10,000.

The old parsonage had been given up as a residence as early as 1828, and ever since Dr. Anthon's settlement in the parish the vestry had made an annual appropriation to defray his house rent. He resided at No. 15 Stuyvesant Street. The old parsonage had recently been thoroughly repaired and painted, but there was a livery stable opposite, which, as Dr. Anthon stated to the vestry, made the location unsuitable for a residence, and the deed of gift provided that if any rector did not choose to live there he might lease it and receive the rent.

The vestry therefore determined to build a rectory on a site agreeable to Dr. Anthon and his family, and No. 156 Second Avenue, on the northeast corner of Tenth Street, was selected. A commodious house was built and furnished and occupied by Dr. Anthon on October 14th, 1840. He notified the vestry of his removal on October 28th, and asked that the record might contain an "expression of the truly grateful feelings entertained by himself and his family for the kindness and liberality which have provided them a residence, in all respects so commodious and complete; their thanks for the confidence and attachment which the vestry have so uniformly and strongly manifested, and their earnest wish and prayer that when the ties which bind us to earthly habitations are sundered they may be renewed forever with his vestry and congregation in the house not made with hands, eternal in the heavens."

In 1845, having been requested by the vestry to deliver an historical discourse on the fiftieth anniversary since the laying of the corner-stone of the church, Dr. Anthon did so, on May 4th. He briefly reviewed the parish history, and then turned to point out its lessons for the future. He dwelt upon the disproportionate increase of the population and the churches. St. Mark's, at his instigation, was ever reaching out a helping hand to needy parishes, and he now broached a plan which in time was put into execution, namely, the erection of a Chapel of Ease. "The seats in such chapels should be free," he said, "and the building under the supervision and control of the same rector and vestry, with the understanding and intention that, at a suitable time, the worshippers should form themselves into a separate and independent congregation. Under judicious counsels, and in economical hands, the enterprise, I am satisfied, is perfectly within the ability of our larger city parishes. Besides the land for the building, it requires but the outlay of a few thousand dollars, and as each rector doubtless would be ready for a time to give voluntary aid, a moderate provision would be needful at the beginning for extra ministerial services."

Toward the end of the year the vestry took steps to learn what could be done to establish such a chapel.

Ever since the reopening of the church, in 1837, dissatisfaction had been expressed with the manner in which the alterations had been made. Fault was found particularly with the decoration of the interior and the retention of the large square pillars supporting the gallery, which obstructed the view of numerous pew-holders. These objections were removed, at a considerable expense, however, the debt having risen to $26,000 in 1846, notwithstanding the sale of several parcels of real estate. The debt was all paid off some ten years later, three lots on Reade Street having been sold for the purpose.

On the 14th of March, 1846, a committee was appointed to consider alterations to the church, and two weeks later they reported that very extensive alterations had been suggested, but that they were "decidedly of opinion that the expenditure of a large sum of money upon the alteration or attempt to the embellishment of an old building is at all times of very questionable expediency, and, as a general rule, should only be incurred when the abundance of means will justify the indulgence of the sentiment of attachment to a favorite or an historical edifice. Unfortunately, the condition of the finances of St. Mark's does not justify the indulgence of any such propensity, if it exist."

They therefore recommended a few slight alterations, as being all that were "absolutely necessary"; and the church was closed from July 20th to October 4th, to be painted and repaired. The condition of the organ had also been under discussion for several years. Of its class, it had been an excellent instrument, but a former organist, to increase its power, as he thought, had almost destroyed it by tampering with the weight on the bellows and the openings of many of the pipes. Many of the ruined parts had since been replaced by new ones, but it was still in a very unsatisfactory condition. The expediency of purchasing a new one was not admitted, however, by all the congregation, and in 1846 a memorial, signed by twenty-seven owners or occupants of pews, including P. G. Stuyvesant, Hamilton Fish and Henry E. Davies, was presented to the vestry. The memorialists represented the danger of a large debt, without any provision for its liquidation, and urged the practice of economy, or the entire property would in time be swallowed up. The vestry did not share these apprehensions, and made a contract with Mr. Henry Erben for a new organ.

On November 18th, 1847, the vestry agreed to the plan that the four neighboring churches— St. Bartholomew's, at the lower end of Lafayette Place; St. Thomas's, on the corner of Broadway and Houston Street; St. Mark's, and the Church of the Ascension—be opened in rotation Sunday evenings.

On Friday, December 10th, 1847, at seven o'clock, the new organ was opened with the following programme:

"Gloria in Excelsis,"
    David R. Harrison, organist of St. Patrick's Cathedral.
Overture to Oberon (Weber),
    William A. King, organist of Grace Church.
Extemporaneous Fantasia,
    George Loder, organist of St. Peter's Church.
Selections from Haydn's Mass, No. 3,
    C. W. Beames, late organist of the Divine Unity.
A Duet, H. W. Greatorex, organist of St. Paul's Church, and
    A. A. Wheeler, organist of Ascension Church.

"Te Deum," or Hymn of Thanksgiving (by Father Lambillotte),
   Wm. Berge, organist of the Church of the Holy Name.
"On Mighty Pinions," from "The Creation" (Haydn),
   M. K. Erben, organist of All Saints' Church.
Select Sacred Airs,
   J. D. Speissegger, organist of St. Mark's Church.
Organ Voluntary,
   H. W. Greatorex.
A Duet,   M. K. Erben and C. W. Beames.

This second organ had three sets of keys, 1,075 pipes, and two octaves of pedals. It cost about $4,500, including the old organ at a valuation of $1,200, and remained in use forty-one years.

During the night of March 1st, 1851, St. Thomas's Church was destroyed by fire, and next day the vestry of St. Mark's met and passed resolutions placing the church at the disposal of the burnt-out congregation for afternoon services. The committee of the vestry of St. Thomas's appointed to return the thanks of their church said: "Should our congregation be obliged to trespass for a time on other churches, there is none to which many of them will turn with more willing feet than to the venerable edifice of St. Mark's, and the sound doctrine of its honored rector."

On May 20th, the repair committee was authorized to have the exterior of the church painted, and at the same meeting steps were taken toward the purchase of a suburban burying ground, as the Common Council had been petitioned to forbid interments in the old cemetery. Offers of large plots were received from

Greenwood Cemetery and the Cemetery of the Evergreens. The latter was accepted, and a plot an acre in extent was purchased and the bodies removed thither from the old cemetery, In order that this might be used for building purposes, the vestry requested Hamilton Fish, himself a descendant of Petrus Stuyvesant through his mother, to procure quitclaims from the legal representatives by inheritance of the said Petrus Stuyvesant, who had given the land in 1803. The releases were all obtained from sixty-one persons scattered through the country from Maine to California.

During the summer of 1855, the ceiling of the church was again painted. On October 12th, 1857, an application was made to the Common Council for two lamp posts in front of the church.

During all the years of Dr. Anthon's rectorship the expenditures for alterations and repairs had been so heavy that his cherished plan of building a mission chapel had been deferred, but now, in 1857, a church on the corner of Second Avenue and Sixth Street was leased for the purpose. After two years this enterprise was given up and another attempt made in what was then spoken of as the northwest quarter of the city, rooms being rented in the Sixth Avenue Railroad building at Forty-fourth Street. This was only temporary, however, for three lots were bought on Forty-eighth Street, between Sixth and Seventh Avenues, and a fine building in the

Italian-Romanesque style, designed by Messrs. Renwick, Auchmuty & Sands, was erected.

In the meantime, in 1858, several important alterations were made about St. Mark's ; the old porch was replaced by one of iron and wood, and the balustrade on the roof and the cornice were added. The church thus assumed its present outward appearance. The stained glass windows which were put in at that time have since been changed, as well as the interior decoration.

The rectorship of Dr. Anthon had now extended almost to its twenty-fifth year. The parish had reached a high level of prosperity during those eventful years, but already the tide of fashion was rolling westward instead of continuing along the then beautiful shore of the East River. Many foreigners were coming into the neighborhood of the church, so that the mission in Sixth Street, with its services in English, was not a success, and St. George's Church determined to start a *German* mission on the East side. In this undertaking Dr. Anthon actively co-operated, proposing the lease of a portion of the old cemetery in Twelfth Street as the site for a chapel, but it was found that this could not be done and the St. George's mission was started on Fourteenth Street.

St. Mark's own chapel in Forty-eighth Street was nearing completion, but Dr. Anthon did not live to see it. He rested from his labors on January 5th, 1861, and on the 8th was buried in one

THE NEW YORK
PUBLIC LIBRARY.

ASTOR, LENOX AND
TILDEN FOUNDATIONS.

of the vaults beside the church. On the 13th, Dr. Tyng preached his funeral sermon.

On January 20th, the vestry resolved to call the Rev. Dr. Alex. H. Vinton, of Holy Trinity Church, Philadelphia, as rector. The call was repeated two weeks later, and on March 5th a report of its acceptance was received.

Dr. Vinton was in his fifty-fourth year, one of the foremost men in the Episcopal Church, and, although an entirely different type of man from his predecessor, one who would surely uphold the traditions of old St. Mark's. His ministry in his last parish was described by Phillips Brooks, who succeeded him there, as "one of the brightest and sunniest pictures which the annals of clerical life have anywhere to show."

On April 4th, 1861, the church in Forty-eighth Street was consecrated as the Memorial Church of the Rev. Henry Anthon, D.D., pursuant to the resolution of St. Mark's vestry, and the Rev. Edward Anthon, who had been his father's assistant since 1856, became its first rector. A mural tablet was erected within the chancel, inscribed as follows :

A MEMORIAL
of the love and esteem of this congregation
for
THE REV. HENRY ANTHON, D.D.,
to whom this church is,
under Divine Providence, indebted
for its existence.

> He rested from his labors
> Jan. 5th, A.D. 1861,
> in the 66th year of his age,
> the 45th of his ministry,
> and the 25th of his rectorship of
> St. Mark's in the Bowery.

> "He was a faithful man,
> And feared God above many."
> Neh. vii. 2.

The land and building were leased to the vestry of the Memorial Church for five years at a nominal rent, with the right to purchase at any time for $12,500, and in 1866 the purchase was made.

St. Mark's did not remain long without a mission chapel, for Dr. Vinton, recognizing the needs of the district east of the church, started one on Avenue A near Eleventh Street, where a room above a feed store was rented. It looked for awhile as if the work would have to be abandoned, so slowly did it prosper, but eventually the accommodations proved too small, and in 1864 certain members of the parish subscribed $10,500, with which a building was purchased on Avenue A, next to the corner of Tenth Street, and fitted up for a mission chapel and school rooms.

In 1866 this work was taken up by the St. Mark's Church in the Bowerie Mission Society, which was incorporated for "the maintenance of religious worship and education among the poor in the city of New York in connexion with the Protestant Episcopal Church in the Diocese of New York." The first board of trustees were the rector of St. Mark's, *ex-officio*, the Rev. Dr. Vinton, and Messrs. Hamilton Fish, Henry B. Renwick, Wm. H. Scott, Peter C. Schuyler, and Alfred H. Easton. The mission received the public commendation of Bishop Horatio Potter before the diocesan convention in 1866.

The wonderful growth of St. Mark's *chapel* shows how the neighborhood was changing, and that a corresponding decline in the *church* was almost inevitable. Dr. Vinton felt that the changing conditions would require a change in the method of administration, but he was now more than sixty years of age, and the outlook for St. Mark's must have appeared rather gloomy to him when he received an invitation to the rectorship of Emmanuel Church, Boston, which he accepted in November, 1869.

During the summer of that year the interior of the church had again been painted, and in 1871 further repairs were made.

Pending the election of a rector, the Rev. Dr. E. O. Flagg was appointed minister-in-charge on April 14th, 1870, and served until Easter, 1871, when Dr. Rylance, who had accepted the rectorship, began his duties. He decided not to occupy the rectory on the corner of Second Avenue and Tenth Street, and took up his residence at No. 11 Livingston Place. Several societies were soon organized, which were fruitful of much good during their existence. Of these "the Literary and Social Reunion," organized 1872, flourished more than twenty years.

The Ladies' Auxiliary Missionary Society, 1874; the Guild of the Good Samaritan, 1876; the Girls' Guild, 1886; the Day Nursery, 1894, have done, and most of them are still doing, much good. The Ladies' Benevolent Society, which remains one of the most active parochial societies, has been in existence since the beginning of Dr. Vinton's rectorship.

In 1881 the old clock, dating back nearly half a century, was replaced by the one still in use.

The work of the Chapel had again outgrown the accommodations when Mr. Rutherfurd Stuyvesant, in 1882, proposed to build a larger and more convenient chapel on the ground occupied by the old building, together with the corner lot, owned by him, provided the administration were lodged in the vestry of St. Mark's Church. This offer was gratefully accepted, and in 1884 the present mission chapel was consecrated. The chapel Sunday-school was temporarily held in Clarendon Hall, Thirteenth Street and Fourth Avenue.

During the summer of 1885 the interior of St. Mark's Church was entirely repainted, and the old chancel rail and the rather plain stained glass windows were replaced by the present ones.

In 1888 the present organ was built by Odell & Co.; it has three sets of keys and 1,992 pipes, and was used for the first time on Sunday

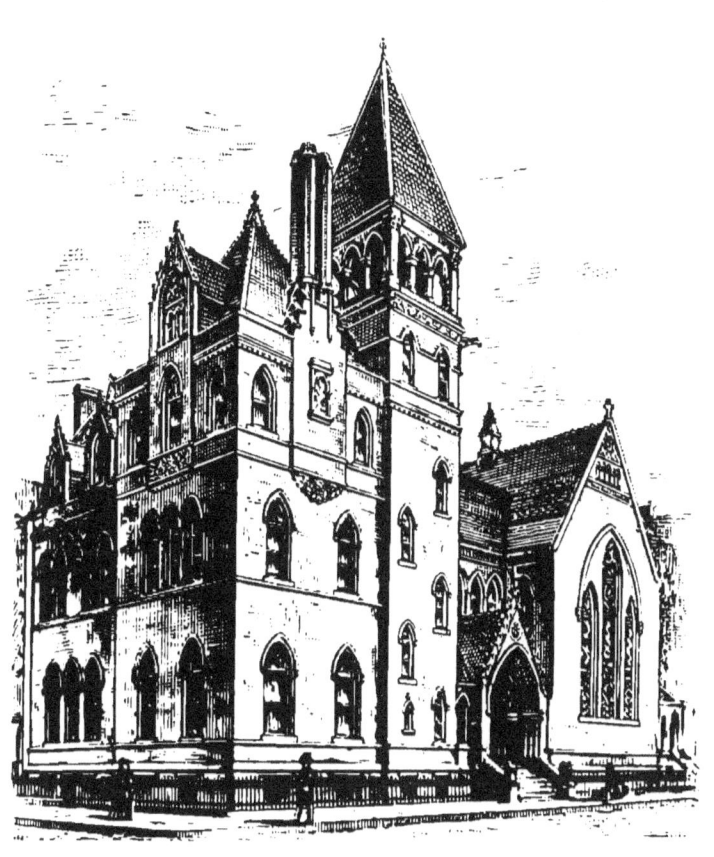

ST. MARK'S CHAPEL
AND PARISH HOUSE.

THE NEW YORK
PUBLIC LIBRARY.

ASTOR, LENOX AND
TILDEN FOUNDATIONS.

October 7th, 1888. The order of services was as follows:

11 A.M.

Processional Hymn, " God, my King, Thy might confessing,"
E. J. Fitzhugh.
Venite, . . . Eighth Tone.
Psalter—8th Selection, . .
Te Deum—Festival, in E flat, . Buck.
Jubilate—E flat, ... Buck.
Introit—Hymn 138, ... Dykes.
Kyrie Eleison, ... Stainer.
Anthem—" How lovely are Thy dwellings," . Spohr.
Sermon.
Ascription—Gloria Patri, . . . Goss.
Offertory Anthem—Quartette—" And be ye kind one to another,"
E. J. Fitzhugh.
Sanctus, ... Eyre.
Communion Hymn—207, . . , Hodges.
Gloria in Excelsis, ... Old Chant.
Recessional—Nunc Dimittis, . . . Barnby.

7:45 P.M.

Processional—" God, my King, Thy might confessing,"
Fitzhugh.
Psalter—Psalm viii.—" O Lord, our Governor," Anglican Chant.
Magnificat—B flat, ... Stainer.
Hymn 424—" All hail the power," . . Old Tune.
The Anthem—Selections from " St. Paul," . Mendelssohn.
Offertory Anthem—Contralto Solo—"Let your thoughts be of heaven," . . . . . Tours.
Doxology.
Recessional—Nunc Dimittis, . . . Stainer.
Postlude (organ)—" Hallelujah Chorus," . . Handel.

On January 9th, 1891, a festoon of the Christmas greens fell upon the lighted gas, and before the fire could be extinguished much damage was done, especially to the new organ, which necessitated closing the church for several months for repairs. At the same time the marble bas-relief over the communion table was erected in place of the painting which formerly occupied that position and a new brass pulpit and reading desk were provided, the latter the gift of the Girls' Guild.

On November 18th, 1898, Dr. Rylance resigned his rectorship, and was made *rector-emeritus*. He had served the church for a longer period than any of his predecessors.

On March 17th, 1899, the vestry arranged with the Rev. Charles Henry Babcock, D.D., to take temporary charge of the parish, several other clergymen having officiated in the meantime.*

This account may fittingly be ended with words which will show how different are the conditions under which the parish starts upon its second century from those under which it began its first. In 1895, on the occasion of the one-hundredth anniversary of the laying of the cornerstone of the church, Dr. Rylance, at the request of the vestry, delivered an historical discourse, at the close of which he described the parochial situation, which the intervening four years have only accentuated.

"Increasing strain is felt," he said, "year by year, from the ever augmenting demands of a populous poor neighborhood, and the loss, through deaths and removals, of means where-

* It should be noted, as this book is going through the press, that on September 1st, the Rev. Loring W. Batten, Ph.D., having accepted a call of the vestry to the rectorate, entered upon the discharge of his duties as the first rector in the church's second century.

with to meet those demands. Steadily and increasingly, wealth betakes itself to inviting retreats, far away ; . . . the moral condition of those parts of our city from which wealth and refinement have so generally fled might become desperate, but for the presence and power within them of our educational institutions, and of our Christian schools and societies. If only to maintain a witness for goodness and purity, therefore, and a protest against vice and irreligion, is it important that our ecclesiastical organizations should retain their hold upon whatever moral vantage ground they now occupy in our crowded poor neighborhoods. St. Mark's Church has been left by the retreating social tide, to a considerable extent, in such a neighborhood, though with lingering traces about us still of its once aristocratic condition, to which the strong, stately mansions that survive carry back the memory of some of us, but which for some time have been in process of transformation into habitations for migratory tenants, or for lodgers,* the process going on visibly before our eyes to-

* The fate of the rectory, which after standing for fifty years, was torn down in 1891, and was replaced by a modern apartment-house with stores, is an illustration in point. Although it was not a "stately mansion," yet, with its old-fashioned gabled roof and dormer windows, it was a quaint reminder of the substantial dwelling of olden times. As it was not in use as a rectory, and was not well situated according to modern requirements, the vestry deemed it expedient to accept an advantageous long lease and consent to its demolition. It is in contemplation to build a rectory on premises recently acquired, adjoining the church's grounds on Eleventh Street.

day. No wonder, how much so ever we may regret the fact, that churches have been compelled to flee from such decaying sections of our community, as from threatening ruin, or that one is made, as so often, to fill the place of two. For even churches cannot subsist for long on sentiment.

"It is an occasion for devout gratitude in all hearts that love this dear old parish, that no material constraint is ever likely to necessitate its removal to any more inviting field—inviting, in a worldly sense of the term, of course; while we may surely hope that those having control of its destiny hereafter will never be tempted to abandon the work of preaching the Gospel to the poor, or of ministering to their necessities, a work than which there is none more blessed, and which Providence has allotted in part to St. Mark's Church; that so, the spot that has been hallowed by memories and associations stretching back across an interval of more than two hundred years may be forever held sacred."

Appendix.

APPENDIX.

Wardens and Vestrymen of St. Mark's Parish from its Foundation to the Present Time.

Wardens.

	FROM	TO
Petrus Stuyvesant	1799	1805
Francis B. Winthrop	1799	1805
Mangle Minthorne	1805	1821
William Ogden	1805	1806
Thomas Ten Eyck	1806	1807
William Ogden	1807	1825
Nicholas Fish	1821	1833
Martin Hoffman	1825	1828
Edward Lyde	1828	1830
Richard I. Tucker	1830	1836
Gideon Lee	1833	1836
John L. Lawrence	1836	1847
Peter G. Stuyvesant	1836	1839
Gerardus Clark	1839	1847
Wheaton Bradish	1847	1861
John Duer	1847	1849
Michael Ulshoeffer	1849	1861
Hamilton Fish	1861	1869
Jacob B. Herrick	1861	1864
Henry B. Renwick	1864	1871
Irving Paris	1869	1875
Peter C. Schuyler	1871	1880
Henry B. Renwick	1875	1895
Hamilton Fish	1880	1884
William Remsen	1884	1890
Edward Coles	1890	1891
Cornelius B. Mitchell	1891	
John Brooks Leavitt	1895	

Vestrymen.

	FROM	TO
Gilbert C. Willett	1799	1802
Martin Hoffman	1799	1825
William A. Hardenbrook	1799	1815
Mangle Minthorne	1799	1805
William Ogden	1799	1805

Name	From	To
George Turnbull	1799	1817
Nicholas W. Stuyvesant	1799	1806
James Cummings	1799	1802
Thomas Ten Eyck	1802	1806
Thomas Bartow	1802	1805
Harry Peters	1805	1808
Anthony Norroway	1805	1816
Nicholas Fish	1805	1821
Robert Bartow	1806	1807
David Mann	1806	1806
Peter G. Stuyvesant	1806	1807
William H. Robinson	1807	1811
John Slidell	1807	1807
Andrew Ogden	1808	1820
Edward Lyde, Jr.	1809	1828
Robert Bird	1811	1813
Dirck Ten Broeck	1813	1819
Noah Talcot	1815	1816
Clement C. Moore	1816	1820
Samuel Ferguson	1816	1817
Michael Ortley	1817	1819
John Day	1817	1818
Peter G. Stuyvesant	1818	1819
David S. Jones	1819	1830
George W. Murray	1819	1821
William Tripler	1819	1825
James Forrest	1820	1830
John W. Kearney	1820	1825
Michael Ortley	1821	1829
Jacob Lorillard	1821	1825
George W. Murray	1825	1826
Peter G. Stuyvesant	1825	1826
Jacob Walton	1825	1830
Gideon Lee	1825	1833
Peter Stuyvesant	1826	1832
Richard I. Tucker	1828	1830
John R. Wheaton	1829	1830
William Neilson	1830	1832
Michael Burnham	1830	1835
Peter Stuyvesant	1830	1831
George Lovett	1830	1835
John L. Ireland	1830	1836
J. Mortimer Catlin	1830	1832
James Gillender	1832	1835
William W. Holly	1832	1835
John L. Lawrence	1832	1839
Christopher Mildeberger	1832	1836
Hamilton Fish	1833	1835
George C. Thomas	1835	1846
James Clinch	1835	1847
Nicholas W. Stuyvesant	1835	1836
Richard L. Morris	1835	1836
Gideon Lee	1836	1837
Richard R. Lansing	1836	1841
Elliot Robins	1836	1838
Wheaton Bradish	1836	1839
Francis U. Johnston	1837	1838

Gerardus Clarke..................................1838....1839
John C. Jay......................................1838 ...1839
John W. Mitchell.................................1839....1844
Francis U. Johnston..............................1839....1844
James Heard......................................1839....1840
Samuel Packwood..................................1839 ...1842
Isaac Carow......................................1840(declined)
Cornelius Du Bois, Jr............................1841....1860
Jacob B. Herrick.................................1841....1861
Hamilton Fish....................................1842....1847
Meigs D. Benjamin................................1844....1846
Samuel S. Rogers.................................1844....1854
Richard L. Morris................................1845....1847
Wheaton Bradish..................................1846....1847
Henry K. Bogert..................................1846....1851
Henry E. Davies..................................1847....1861
John S. Heard....................................1847....1857
Edward S. Gould..................................1847....1848
Michael Ulshoeffer...............................1848....1849
William Scott....................................1848....1851
Gerard Stuyvesant................................1849....1859
Augustus H. Ward.................................1851....1854
Nathan Babcock...................................1851....1855
John M. Catlin...................................1854....1860
Thomas B. Dibblee................................1854....1860
Ambrose L. Jordan................................1855 ...1860
Henry B. Renwick.................................1857....1864
Thomas McMullen..................................1859....1864
Irving Paris.....................................1860....1869
James Colles.....................................1860....1864
William Remsen...................................1860....1884
Thomas M. Beare..................................1860....1865
Meigs D. Benjamin................................1861....1866
Peter C. Schuyler................................1861....1871
Alfred H. Easton.................................1864....1867
Albert G. Thorp, Jr..............................1864....1866
William H. Scott.................................1864....1872
Edward B. Wesley.................................1865....1870
William K. Kitchen...............................1866....1869
Grant Thorburn...................................1866....1868
James Purdon.....................................1867....1887
Robert J. Hubbard................................1868....1869
James Morris.....................................1869....1871
George H. Morgan.................................1869....1873
Edward Oothout...................................1870....1681
Nicholas W. S. Catlin............................1870....1890
John W. Chanler..................................1871....1873
William T. Lawrence..............................1871....1874
Henry B. Renwick.................................1872....1875
William H. Scott.................................1873....1877
Rutherfurd Stuyvesant............................1873....1890
Evert A. Duyckinck...............................1874....1879
Allen J. Cuming..................................1875....1883
John H. Iselin...................................1877....1880
Robert Stuyvesant................................1879....1884
William V. King..................................1880....1890
Stuyvesant F. Morris.............................1881.....1890

Joseph A. Dean	1883	1884
H. Duncan Wood	1884	1885
Hamilton Fish, Jr	1884	1890
Charles C. Peck	1884	1890
William A. Sackett	1885	1890
Francis B. Austen	1887	1890
David Lydig	1890	1891
Charles W. Muzio	1890	1892
William R. Carr	1890	1893
Charles C. Kross	1890	1894
James L. Bishop	1890	1894
Cornelius B. Mitchell	1890	1891
Henry E. Coe	1890	1893
John Herriman, Jr	1890	
Edward O. Coles	1891	1898
John Brooks Leavitt	1891	1895
Charles G. Cornell, Jr	1892	1897
Henry A. Simonds	1893	
Zelah Van Loan	1893	
H. Duncan Wood	1894	1898
William F. Beller	1894	
Lewis B. Moore	1895	
Charles E. Goodhue	1897	
William F. Simpson	1898	1899
George W. Clark	1898	
David Lydig	1899	

Treasurers of the Vestry.

	FROM	TO
William A. Hardenbrook	1799	1805
Martin Hoffman	1805	1825
Edward Lyde	1825	1828
Gideon Lee	1828	1836
George C. Thomas	1836	1842
Jacob B. Herrick	1842	1863
Hamilton Fish	1863	1865
Edward B. Wesley	1865	1870
Irving Paris	1870	1875
Allen J. Cumming	1875	1883
James Purdon	1883	1887
William V. King	1887	1890
Charles C. Kross	1890	1894
Zelah Van Loan	1894	

Clerks of the Vestry.

	FROM	TO
Peter Gerard Stuyvesant	1799	1802
Martin Hoffman	1802	1805
Nicholas Fish	1805	1821
Edward Lyde	1821	1825
David S. Jones	1825	1830
John Mortimer Catlin	1830	1832
John L. Lawrence	1832	1836

Hamilton Fish......................................1836....1839
John W. Mitchell..................................1839....1844
Hamilton Fish.....................................1844....1847
Cornelius Dubois..................................1847....1849
John S. Heard.....................................1849....1857
Thomas B. Dibblee.................................1857....1858
Henry B. Renwick..................................1858....1865
Irving Paris......................................1865....1870
William Remsen....................................1870....1871
N. W. Stuyvesant Catlin...........................1871 ...1890
Henry E. Coe......................................1890 ...1893
Charles G. Cornell, Jr............................1893....1897
Lewis B. Moore....................................1897....1899
William F. Beller.................................1899 ....

Pewholders at Different Periods.

A list of the first pewholders of St. Mark's Church with the annual rent under a five-year lease.

The sale took place Wednesday, October 2nd, 1799.

PEW NUMBER.		SHILLINGS.
30	Nicholas W. Stuyvesant	40
31	Hezekiah Rogers	30
32	Samuel Hallett	45
33	James Bleecker	56
34	Anthony L. Bleecker	46
35	William A. Hardenbrook	110
36		40
37	George Turnbull	
38		35
39	Martin Hoffman	32
40	James Seton	30
43	Edward Lyde	34
44	John Jones	43
45	William Ogden	60
46	Horatio Gates	60
47	Francis B. Winthrop	60
48	R. T. Kemble	60
49	John Slidell	52
50	John Ireland	32
66	James Jarvis	32
67	George Scroeppell	37
68	Thomas Ten Eyck	44
69	Mr. Overling	56
70	Robert Bird	78
71	Nicholas Fish	74
72	Gilbert Colden Willett	71
73	William A. Hardenbrook	61
74	Captain Smith	43
75	Abijah Hibbard	31
77	John Pell	51
78	Nicholas Carmer	60
79	Thomas B. Bridgen	70
80	Mr. Buchanan	51
82	William Thomas	140
83	James A. Stewart	50
84	Robert Benson	44
85	Daniel Kemper	44
86	David Williamson	34

On October 8th, the Clerk reported the sale of six additional pews.

2	John Bleecker	64
6	Hugh Gaine	40

PEW NUMBER.		SHILLINGS.
42	Jane Shaw	40
51	Thomas Bartow	40
52	Mr. Schifflin	40
109	Mr. Cadle	40

A list of the lessees at the second sale of pews, held on Saturday, August 4th, 1804, under a seven-year lease, with the annual rent.

PEW NUMBER.		ANNUAL RENT.	
2	Miss Dow	$ 9	50
6	Hugh Gaine	6	00
7	Mrs. McVickar	9	00
8	Mrs. Rogers	12	50
10, 11, 12.	William Bayard	14	50
13, 14.	David Dunham	7	50
30	Benjamin Winthrop	8	00
31	Hezekiah Rogers	5	00
32	Peter G. Stuyvesant	5	00
33, 34.	Anthony L. Bleecker	10	00
35	William A. Hardenbrook	20	00
36	M. Hoffman	5	00
37	George Turnbull	5	00
38	David Mann	6	00
42	Mrs. Jane Shaw	6	00
43	Edward Lyde	7	50
44	John Jones	13	00
45	William Ogden	20	00
46	General Gates	25	50
47	F. B. Winthrop	18	00
48	R. T. Kemble	18	00
49	John Slidell	15	00
50	John Ireland	11	00
51	Joseph Waddington	7	00
52	John Jones	6	00
66	George Barnard	8	00
67	George Scroeppell	11	00
68	Mr. Cadle	14	00
69	Thomas Ten Eyck	17	00
70	Edmund Hanson	23	00
71	Nicholas Fish	23	00
72	Archibald Grain	24	00
73	William Renwick	25	00
74	Henry Peters	11	00
75	James Forrester	9	50
76	Oliver Waldron	5	00
78	R. Lenox	6	00
79	Dirck Ten Broeck	8	00
80	Nathaniel Bell	4	00
81	Mangle Minthorne	5	00
82	William Thomas	15	00
83	George Warner	10	00
84, 85.	R. Bartow	12	50
86	David Williamson	6	00
105, 106, 107.	James Farquhar	12	50
108	N. W. Stuyvesant	19	00
109	Mr. Cadle	4	00

PEW NUMBER.	ANNUAL RENT.
111....Mr. Brady	$ 6 00
112....John Pell	9 50
116....Bishop Moore	10 00

In 1811, when the second leases expired, the vestry
"*Resolved:* That the pewholders, after the expiration of their present leases, have the privilege of renewing the same for the term of seven years, subject to the payment of the same purchase money and annual rent as heretofore, and that the pew committee be authorized to dispose of any pews which may be surrendered, in like manner as if retained by the present holders."
The following pews were at once taken:

PEW NUMBER.

- 32....Mrs. Pollock.
- 33, 34. Robert Bird.
- 36....Martin Hoffman.
- 37....George Turnbull.
- 38....Widow Mann.
- 43....Edward Lyde.
- 44....Nathaniel Lawrence.
- 45....William Ogden.
- 48....Jonathan Ogden.
- 50....John Ireland.
- 67....George Schroeppell.
- 68....Andrew Ogden.
- 71....Nicholas Fish.
- 74....Edmund Morewood.
- 81....Mangle Minthorne.
- 82....William Thomas.
- 108....Nicholas W. Stuyvesant.
- 111....Mrs. Brady.

Other pews were taken from time to time until, in 1816, near the end of the seven years, the pewholders were:

- 1....The Rector.
- 9....Mrs. Stuyvesant.
- 30....Benjamin Winthrop.
- 31....George Newbold.
- 32....Mrs. Pollock.
- 33....Thomas Tripler.
- 34....Samuel Hallett.
- 35....Mr. Farquhar.
- 36....Martin Hoffman.
- 37....George Turnbull.
- 39....Mrs. Staples.
- 40....William Wilmerding.
- 42....Mrs. Shaw.
- 43....Edward Lyde.
- 44....Nathaniel Lawrence.
- 45....William Ogden.
- 46....Mr. Walsh.
- 48....Clement C. Moore.
- 49....Mr. Johnson.
- 50... John Ireland.
- 65, 66. Mrs. Byron.
- 67.. George Schroeppell.
- 68....Andrew Ogden.
- 69....Thomas Brantingham.
- 70....Wm. L. Hull.
- 71....Nicholas Fish.
- 72....David S. Jones.
- 73....John Day.
- 74....Edmund Morewood.
- 75....James Forrest.
- 76....Oliver Waldron.
- 78....William Inman.
- 79....Dirck Ten Broeck.
- 81....Mangle Minthorne.
- 82....Mrs. Thomas.
- 84....Judah Hammond.
- 85....Noah Talcott.
- 86....Joseph Rose.
- 87....George Ironside.
- 88....Henry Ritter.
- 108....Nicholas W. Stuyvesant.
- 111....Mrs. Brady.
- 115....Michael Ortley.

In 1837 the policy of leasing the pews for seven years was abandoned, and on May 11th a public auction was held in the church, at which twenty-seven pews were sold in perpetuity at the prices and subject to the annual rents named below.

PEW NUMBER.	PURCHASER.	PRICE.	ANNUAL RENT.
1....Peter G. Stuyvesant		$405	$24
2....Mrs. Martha Babcock		405	24

PEW NUMBER.	PURCHASER.	PRICE.	ANNUAL RENT.
3	Richard R. Lansing	$405	$24
5	The Misses Corré	325	24
12	Meigs D. Benjamin	300	22
17	Mrs. C. Pratt	200	18
31	B. R. Winthrop	650	30
35	Reuben Withers	700	30
36	B. R. Winthrop	410	24
37	Cornelius Dubois	400	24
40	James Heard	600	30
43	Samuel Packwood	505	25
45	E. F. Sanderson	500	25
65	C. Bartlett	515	25
66	Mrs. Fish	510	25
67	Dr. R. L. Morris	505	25
68	H. Fish	500	25
81	Peter G. Stuyvesant	600	30
74	Wheaton Bradish	405	24
75	Peter Stuyvesant	400	24
76	Robert Van Rensselaer	705	30
77	J. M. Catlin	405	24
80	John L. Lawrence	650	30
89	William W. Thomas	100	15
94	Henry Wilkes	200	18
107	G. C. Thomas	435	30
111	Peter G. Stuyvesant	50	5

In addition the following pews were disposed of at private sale:

47	Stanton Parker	$550	$25
64	Gerardus Clark	500	25
70	John L. Graham	500	25
79	Thomas Dean	400	24

On Wednesday afternoon, April 18th, 1838, at four o'clock, another auction sale of pews was held in St. Mark's Church, at which the following twenty pews were sold:

PEW NUMBER.	PURCHASER.	ANNUAL RENT.
8	P. G. Stuyvesant	$22
14, 15	M. D. Benjamin	36
22	G. C. Thomas	15
32	A. T. Stewart	24
33	J. H. Ward	24
34	D. Jackson	24
38	James L. Graham	24
42	John Anthon	25
44	Isaac Carow	25
46	T. S. McCarthy	25
62	C. Mildaberger	25
69	E. S. Gould	25
73	P. G. Stuyvesant	25
97	Mr. Meredith	22
102	H. E. Davies	22
103	T. J. Davies	22
106	Dr. Pennell	25
109	Mrs. J. H. Smith	24
152	Charles Marsh	6

Twelve additional pews were subsequently sold as follows:

PEW NUMBER.	PURCHASER.	PEW NUMBER.	PURCHASER.
7	Cornelius Du Bois.	63	Edwin Bergh.
16	J. W. G. Clements.	78	R. R. Stuyvesant.
20	Mr. Wilson.	81	A. N. Lawrence.
30	William Remsen.	85	C. L. Carpenter.
39	P. C. Schuyler.	101	T. H. Morgan.
52	S. J. Tyler.	104	Ogden Haggerty.

The following is a list of all who owned or rented pews in 1845, when Dr. Anthon preached his jubilee sermon:

1.... P. G. Stuyvesant.
2.... Mrs. M. Babcock.
3.... Russell and Lowden.
4.... The Rector's family.
5.... The Misses Corré.
6.... H. P. Hubbell.
7.... Cornelius Du Bois.
8, 9, 10, 11. P. G. Stuyvesant.
12.... F. V. Johnston.
13.... J. W. Mitchell.
14, 15. M. D. Benjamin.
16.... N. Pearce.
17.... Mrs. C. Pratt.
18.... Lemuel Arnold.
19.... B. D. Breeck.
20.... J. A. Smith.
21.... G. L. Brown.
22.... G. C. Thomas.
23.... John Redmond.
24.... Edward Godfrey.
25.... James Maxwell.
26.... J. F. Waldron.
27.... Mrs. Lawrence.
28.... A. C. Baldwin.
29.... Mrs. Eigdenbrod.
30.... Mrs. J. Suydam.
31.... B. R. Winthrop.
32.... A. T. Stewart.
33.... A. H. Ward.
34.... Henry Harbeck.
35.... Reuben Withers.
36.... B. R. Winthrop.
37.... Cornelius Du Bois.
38.... James L. Graham.
39.... N. Babcock.
40.... James Heard.
41.... Edward Willis.
42.... John Anthon.
43.... Samuel Packwood.
44.... Isaac Carow.
45 ... E. F. Sanderson.
46.... Mrs. T. McCarty.
47.... Estate of S. Parker.
48.... D. F. Manice.
49.... Samuel Sherwood.
50.... Elijah Paine.
51.... S. F. Barry.
52.... J. B. Herrick.
53.... R. W. Wood.
54.... Mrs. Anderson.
55.... Clark Greenwood.
56.... J. W. Richardson.
58.... Watson Lawrence.
59.... Dr. Manley.
60.... William Small.
61.... Lemuel Smith.
62.... C. Mildaberger.
63.... C. S. Hubbard.
64.... Gerardus Clark.
65.... C. Bartlett.
66.... Mrs. N. Fish.
67.... Dr. Morris.
68.... Hamilton Fish.
69.... E. S. Gould.
70.... J. L. Graham.
71.... P. G. Stuyvesant.
72.... James Heard.
73.... G. Stuyvesant.
74.... W. Bradish.
75, 76. N. W. Stuyvesant.
77.. Mrs. M. Spingler.
78.... G. Stuyvesant.
79.... Thomas Dean.
80.... J. L. Lawrence.
81.... William Chadwick.
82.... Samuel Rogers.
83.... Charles Easton.
84.... Cook and Holbrook.
85.... Mrs. Hoyt.
86.... J. H. Guion.
87.... A. A. Leggett.
88.... William Herrington.
89.... W. W. Thomas.
90.... Mr. Pomeroy.
91.... J. B. Moreau.
92.... A. N. Lawrence.
93.... J. C. Thatcher.
94.... H. Wilkes.

95....W. B. Pinckney.
96....W. H. Pinckney.
97....A. N. Lawrence.
98....Charles Purviance.
99....Dr. Marcellin.
100....N. Stuyvesant.
101....J. L. Morgan.
102....H. Davis.
103....Ogden Haggerty.
104....H. Ludlow.
105....R. Pennell.
106....H. Kneeland.
107....G. C. Thomas.
109....W. R. Smith.
110....John Duer.
111....P. G. Stuyvesant.
112....Samuel Scott.
113, 114. Mrs. L. Mitchell.
115....W. Bradish.
120....John Ruderson.
121....W. Dibblee.
126....Samuel Wetmore.
141... O. Stebbins.
143....W. Blake.
145....W. B. Shipman.
146....W. D. Disbrow.
147....J. C. Clarkson.
150....P. E. Berkhead.
151....Edward Martin.
152....Charles Marsh.
153....T. B. Wakeman.
156....C. L. Carpenter.

During the past few years, the vestry, realizing that altered conditions might render it desirable to change to free sittings, have pursued the policy of regaining title to pews. Some have been generously presented by their owners as free pews forever. The number of ground-rent pews is now small and is as follows:

1....Robert R. Stuyvesant.
7....David Lydig.
15....Estate of Geo. E. White.
30....Elizabeth Remsen.
31....Egerton Winthrop.
32....Estate of A. T. Stewart.
33....   "   " A. Warner.
36....Egerton Winthrop.
42....Estate of Sarah N. Smith.
43....   "   " J. W. Chanler.
48....E. B. Wesley.
64....Estate of H. W. Clark.
66....Mrs. E. S. Howard.
67....James Morris.
68....Estate of Hamilton Fish.
71....   "   " Hamilton Fish.
73....Robert R. Stuyvesant.
74....Estate of Mrs. Fonerden.
75....Robert Stuyvesant.
76....Estate of N. S. W. Catlin.
77....   "   " Mrs. Fonerden.
78....Robert R. Stuyvesant.
80....Estate of J. Lawrence.
81....Hannah N. Lawrence.
85....Estate of C. L. Carpenter.
94....   "   " S. H. Cornell.
102....   "   " Henry E. Davies.
111....Rutherfurd Stuyvesant.

Assistant Ministers in Charge of the Chapel.

Rev. Edward Anthon, 1856–1861.
Rev. Samuel Maxwell, 1861-2.
Rev. George W. Foote, 1864-5.
Rev. Thomas R. Harris, 1866-7.
Rev. Walter Delafield, 1867-8.
Rev. Justin P. Kellogg, 1869.
Rev. James P. Franks, 1870.
Rev. Albert Sidney Dealey, 1871.
Rev. Albert W. Snyder, 1872.
Rev. Stephen A. McNulty, 1874-6.
Rev. Henry B. Ensworth, 1876-9.
Rev. Brockholst Morgan, 1880-4.
Rev. John E. Johnson, 1885-7.
Rev. Laurence H. Schwab, 1887-8.
Rev. Nathaniel L. Briggs, 1890-1.
Rev. Charles G. Adams, 1891-3.
Rev. Richard Cobden, 1893-7.
Rev. Walter E. Bentley, 1897-9.
Rev. Rudolph M. Binder, 1899.

Organists.

1824-5	Michael K. Erben.	1861	T. M. Tyng.
1825-30	Thomas Hall.	1862	William A. King.
1830	A. Taylor.	1863	Edward J. Connelly.
1830-2	R. S. Williams.	1864-5	John N. Pattison.
1832	John Greenwood.	1865-8	Charles Wels.
1833	Charles Heidelberg.	1869-72	Joseph H. Guild.
1834-46	James D. Walton, Jr.	1874-9	W. E. Beames.
1846	{ George H. Curtis. Mr. Pearson. W. T. Berry.	1881-2	{ Mr. Nieudorf. Mr. Muller.
		1882	Augustine Cortada.
1846-7	John D. Speissegger.	1883-4	S. N. Penfield.
1848-9	Clare M. Beames.	1885-92	E. J. Fitzhugh.
1850-3	William R. Bristow.	1892-99	William Edward Mulligan.
1853-59	Louis Schmidt.	1899	Willis H. Alling.
1859-60	William H. Milnor.		

The Organs.

First organ built 1823, by Thomas Hall; enlarged 1825.
Second organ built 1847, by Henry Erben.
Third organ, built 1888, by J. H. & C. S. Odell & Co.

Sextons of St. Mark's Church.

	FROM	TO
Luke Kip	1799	1801
Asa L. French	1801	1802
Frederick Rigur	1802	1806
Stephen Palmer	1806	1808
Hezekiah Rogers	1808	1811
Isaac Wilkins	1811	1825
William D. Disbrow	1825	1848
Charles L. Carpenter	1848	1869
George W. Hamill	1869	1896
James H. Lewis	1896	

Memorial Tablets in St. Mark's Church.

Chancel.

Within the chancel recess are two tablets, both of white marble, on a background of black variegated marble, with inscriptions in black letters.

On the western side:

Sacred to the memory of the REV. JOHN CALLAHAN, Minister of this Church, who, on a visit to his Parents and Friends at Charleston, South Carolina, was thrown out of a Carriage, and expired the same day, April 14, 1800, Æ 24.
This tribute of esteem and affection for departed worth is erected by the Vestry of this Church.

His spirit's fled! and reigns above,
In realms of joy, of peace, of love,
And death has done his part!
Why rear a tomb, a splendid tomb,
To give his name to years to come?
When rear'd it's in the heart.

On the eastern side:

To the memory of
PETER STUYVESANT.
This monument is erected by his children
as a testimony of
filial Love and Gratitude.
He was born 13th October, 1727, O. S.,
Died 7th October, 1805,
And his remains are deposited
in the vault of his Ancestors
within the walls of this Church.
The kind Father, the faithful Friend,
The honest Citizen, and the sincere Christian
rests from his Labours,
and his Works do follow him.

North Wall.

East of the chancel, above the door, is a white marble tablet on a black marble background, with the inscription in black, and a portrait bust in relief at the top:

The
Wardens and Vestrymen
of
St. Mark's Church in the Bowery

have erected
this tablet
to the memory of
the REV. HENRY ANTHON, D.D.,
who was born March 11, 1795,
Ordained September 29, 1816,
chosen rector of this church January 14, 1837,
and departed this life January 5, 1861.

A faithful minister of the Lord Jesus Christ,
a devoted son of the Protestant Episcopal Church,
a Catholic Christian, a good Citizen, an honest man.
His life was an example of singular purity and consistency.
As he lived and labored for Christ,
so he died in the full faith and hope of His Gospel.

"*He was a faithful man, and feared God above many.*"—NEHEMIAH 7, 2.

Under the gallery, between the door and the eastern wall, is a white marble tablet on a white background, with the following inscription in black:

Sacred to the memory
of
PETER SCHERMERHORN.
Died 28th January, 1826,
aged 76 years.
And of
ELIZABETH SCHERMERHORN,
wife of
Peter Schermerhorn.
Died 8th January, 1809,
aged 56 years.
Their remains are deposited in the family vault in
the cemetery of this church.

Under the gallery, between the door and the western wall, is a black marble tablet in a white marble frame, with inscription in gold letters:

SAMUEL FERGUSON.
Born
April 11, 1769,
At Halifax, in England.
Died
August 2, 1816, at New York.
And his wife
ELIZABETH.
Born
July 4, 1778,
In the County of Suffolk, England.
Died
October 6, 1823, at New York.
This Tablet is erected
by
their affectionate children
to perpetuate the memory
of the Dead

and
the Gratitude of the Living.
Their remains are deposited in a vault in the
Cemetery attached to this Church.

East Wall.

On the eastern wall under the gallery are four tablets as follows, beginning at the front:
Between the first and second windows, a white marble tablet on a black background, with inscription in black:

NICHOLAS FISH,
Lieut.-Colonel in the Army of the American Revolution.
Born August 28, 1758.
Died June 20, 1833.
The faithful soldier of Christ and of his country.

Below is a brass tablet on a black marble background:
In memory of
ELIZABETH, daughter of Petrus Stuyvesant,
Wife of Nicholas Fish.
Born February 11, 1775. Passed from death into life
September 6, 1854.
Steadfast in faith, joyful through hope, rooted in charity; Perfect in every relation of Child, Wife, Mother, Neighbour and Friend.

Between the second and third windows, a full-length white marble figure of Faith in high relief in an arched recess. On the tablet below in black:
Faith,
Integrity and Sincerity distinguished
the character of
PETER GERARD STUYVESANT,
who was called suddenly to life eternal
August 16, 1847, aged 69 years.

"Be ye also ready, for in such an hour as ye think not, the Son of Man cometh."

Between the third and fourth windows, a white marble tablet on black background, with inscription in black:
Sacred
to the memory
of
JACOB B. HERRICK.
Born Sept. 6, 1800. Died Jan. 2, 1864.
Senior Warden. And for more than
twenty years Treasurer of this church.
With a gentle, affectionate and sympathizing nature, he combined integrity, firmness and decision of character.

These qualities, sanctified by grace, made him the humble Christian, the valued friend and the worthy citizen.

He died, having the testimony of a good conscience, in the communion of the Catholic Church, in the confidence of a certain faith, in the comfort of a reasonable religious and holy hope, in favor with God and in perfect charity with the world.

West Wall.

On the western wall under the gallery are four tablets, as follows, beginning at the front:

Between the first and second windows, a white marble tablet on a black marble background, with inscription in black:

Erected to the memory
of
GEORGE TURNBULL,
Post-Captain in the
British Navy,
Who died in New York, Nov. 13, 1825,
Aged 82 years.
And of
MARGARET,
His wife,
Who died at Beccles, England,
Jan. 22, 1829,
Aged 72 years.
Also
WILLIAM P. TURNBULL
and
GEORGE TURNBULL, JR.,
Who were born in New York;
The Former on the 3d November, 1791;
The Latter on the 1st December, 1800.
And who sailed from Smyrna in the brig Minerva,
On their return home, in the latter part of the year 1821,
And of which vessel no account has been received.

"And God shall wipe away all tears from their eyes; and there shall be no more death, neither sorrow, nor crying, neither shall there be any more pain, for the former things are passed away."—REV. xxi. 4.

Between the second and third windows, a white marble tablet on a black marble background, with inscription in black:

In
memory of
CATHERINE,
wife of
John R. Stuyvesant.
Born October 25, 1808.
Died November 17, 1837.

Between the third and fourth windows, a white marble tablet on a black marble background, with inscription in black:

In
memory of
WILLIAM H. PINKNEY.
Died June 17th, 1850,
Aged 68 years, 7 months
and 3 days.
Also of his wife,
HANNAH BERTINE.
Died
November 14th, 1843,
Aged 53 years, 9 months
and 14 days.

———

"*This mortal must put on immortality.*"

———

Between the fourth and fifth windows, a large brass tablet on black marble background:

To the Glory of God
and in memory of
ALEXANDER H. VINTON, D.D.
Born May 2nd, 1807.
Died April 26th, 1881.
Rector of this parish of St. Mark
From 1861 to 1869.

———

"*We preach not ourselves, but Christ Jesus the Lord,
And ourselves your servants for Jesus' sake.*"

———

South Wall.

On the rear wall, between the middle and eastern door, is a brass tablet with a floral border in red and black, on a black marble background:

In affectionate remembrance of
FANNIE BOZEMAN RYLANCE.
Erected by the Girls' Guild and Sunday School of St. Mark's Church,
Easter, 1895.

———

"*Thrice blest whose lives are faithful prayers:
Whose loves in higher love endures.*"

———

Vestibule.

On the eastern side of the middle vestibule is a brass tablet on a variegated marble background, in the shape of a Greek cross, with an anchor in the upper limb:

In loving remembrance of
CHARLES HENRY BALDWIN,
Rear-Admiral United States Navy.
Born September 3d, 1822.
Died November 17th, 1888.
Safe in Port.

THE NEW YORK
PUBLIC LIBRARY.

ASTOR, LENOX AND
TILDEN FOUNDATIONS.

PETRUS STUYVESANT'S TOMB.

In Pews.

Pews Nos. 35 and 40 bear brass plates with the following inscriptions:

No. 35.
In memory of
REUBEN AND MATILDA A. WITHERS,
Occupants of this pew for many years.
Donated to St. Mark's Church, as a free pew forever,
By their daughter,
VIRGINIA M. PAINE.

No. 40.
In memory of
PETER C. AND HANNAH C. SCHUYLER,
Owners of this pew for many years.
Presented to
St. Mark's Church
As a free pew forever.

Tablets on the Exterior of the Church.

On the eastern wall under the second window from the porch:

In this vault lies buried
PETRUS STUYVESANT,
late Captain-General and Governor-in-chief of Amsterdam
in New Netherland, now called New York,
and the Dutch West India Islands, died in A.D. 167$\frac{1}{2}$,*
aged 80 years.

On the rear wall:
Sacred
to the memory of
JOHN ANDREW BOULTON,
late
of York in Upper Canada.
Born July 4th, 1810.
Died October 2nd, 1829.
Interred
in vault No. 52 at St. Mark's Church.

---

* The date of Governor Stuyvesant's death, given on his tombstone as 167$\frac{1}{2}$, is on account of the old and new style. In England, until 1753, the legal year began on March 25th, so that all dates between January 1st and March 25th fell into different years, according to the style employed. Governor Stuyvesant died in February, 1671, according to the old style, 1672 according to the new.

In the same vault reposes the body of the English governor, Col. Henry Sloughter, who died in 1691.

This
monument
is erected to the memory of
JANE AMANDA,
who died June 20th, 1827,
aged 1 year,
0 months and 17 days;
also
JOSEPH SMITH,
who died January 17th, 1834,
aged 4 days;
and
JANE DYAS,
who died Sept. 11th, 1835,
aged 4 years,
3 months and 13 days.
The children of
Jane Amanda Perry
and
Joseph Smith.
Interred in vault No. 32.

On the rear wall of the Sunday-school building:

Erected
to the memory of my
Beloved Mother,
SUSAN MABEE,
who died
Nov. 8th, 1849,
Aged 71 years.

Effaced from her meek brow all
  Lines of sickness, grief and care,
And placid as a sleeping child
  She lay in beauty there.
While round her lips, on which
  Had dwelt the holy law of love,
Lingered a sweet, celestial smile,
  Type of the peace above.
Our mother dear, tho' changes
  Come and time swift onward rolls,
Yet thou shall live unchanging,
  Still enshrined within our souls,
When tempted, and when sorely
  Tried, our spirits then will turn
To thy meek virtues, embalmed
  In memory's priceless urn.

Near this spot
repose
the dear and beloved remains
of

GEORGE MANNERS BARTLETT,
son of
John S. and Martha Bartlett,
of this City,
whose pure spirit departed from
this transitory world
Dec. 31st, 1856,
in the 19th year of his age.
This Tablet
is erected by his
Affectionate Parents
as a memento of their affection
for a
Good Dutiful Son,
and to preserve these his last words,
REMEMBER ME.

Memorial Windows.

The Stuyvesant Window.

The second window from the front on the east side:
The Angel of the Resurrection.
Inscription below:
"WHY SEEK YE THE LIVING AMONG THE DEAD? HE IS NOT HERE, BUT IS RISEN."
In lower left hand corner—monogram M. R. S.
In lower right hand corner—1879.
This window was erected by Mr. Rutherfurd Stuyvesant to the memory of his wife.

The Winthrop Window.

Third window from the front on the east side. St. Mark. Inscription, in scrolls above, *Spes vincit thronum. Jovae praestat fidere quam homini.*

On the left side:

PETER WILLIAM.
Nat., 25th September, 1787.
Obt., 23rd February, 1814.

EGERTON LEIGH.
Nat., 5th July, 1792.
Obt., 30th November, 1834.

GERARD STUYVESANT.
Nat., 14th August, 1796.
Obt., 10th November, 1829.

MARGARET CORNELIA.
Nat., 22nd July, 1801.
Obt., 18th March, 1863.
M., George Folsom.

On the right side:

ELIZABETH SHIRREFF.
Nat., 4th October, 1789.
Obt., 28th December, 1866.
M., Rev. John W. Chanler.

BENJAMIN ROBERT.
Nat., 24th September, 1794.
Obt., 10th September, 1800.

JOHN HAY.
Nat., 29th November, 1798.
Obt., 29th April, 1840.

BENJAMIN ROBERT.
Nat., 18th January, 1804.
Obt., London, Eng., 26th July, 1879.

ELIZA ANN COLES NEILSON.
Nat., 31st July, 1880.
Obt., 27th February, 1891.

Below the evangelist, St. Mark:

On the left side:
In memory of
BENJAMIN WINTHROP.
Nat., New London, Connecticut, 17th September, 1762.
Obt., City of New York, 9th January, 1844.

On the right side:
In memory of
JUDITH WINTHROP,
Wife of Benjamin Winthrop, Daughter of Petrus Stuyvesant.
Nat., New York, 25th December, 1765.
Obt., 7th March, 1844.

The Hamill Window.

The fifth window on the east side:
The Call of St. Peter.
Inscription below:
To the glory of God and in loving memory of
GEORGE W. HAMILL. 1834-1896. Erected by his children.

*"Lord, I have loved the habitation of thy house,
and the place where thine honour dwelleth."*

The Weston Window.

The first from the front on the west side:
Mary sitting at the feet of Jesus.
Inscription in scroll above to the left:
"MARY SAT AT JESUS' FEET."
Inscription in scroll above to the right:
"AND HEARD HIS WORDS."
Inscription below:
In
memory
of
MARY CATHARINE NORTH,
wife of Rev. D. C. Weston, D.D.
Died August 4th, 1882.

The Lawrence Window.

The second window on the west side:
St. John the Divine.
Inscription below:
"FROM HENCEFORTH BLESSED ARE THE DEAD
WHO DIE IN THE LORD; EVEN SO, SAITH THE
SPIRIT, FOR THEY REST FROM THEIR LABORS."

In memory of
JOHN L. LAWRENCE.
Born October 2nd,
1785. Died
July 24th, 1849.

In memory of
SARAH AUSTIN,
wife of John L.
Lawrence. Born
May 19th, 1794.
Died Nov. 13th, 1877.

The Pinkney Window.

The fourth on the west side.
Christ Blessing the Children.
Inscription below:
"SUFFER LITTLE CHILDREN TO COME UNTO ME."
WILLIAM H. PINKNEY.
HANNAH PINKNEY.
MILLARD GLENN TILLOTSON.

The Richardson Window.

The fifth window on the west side:
>*St. Augustine.*

Inscription in scrolls on either side:

ANN RICHARDSON,	Passed away
wife of	11th of July
J. Richardson.	A.D. 1872.

Inscription below: ST. AUGUSTINE.
Below on each side—a coat-of-arms.

The Sunday-school Window.

In the Sunday-school room:
>*Christ Blessing the Children.*

Inscription below:
"HE PUT HIS HANDS ON THEM AND BLESSED THEM."

At the bottom on two scrolls:
>IN LOVING MEMORY OF TEACHERS AND SCHOLARS
>AT REST.
>THE GIFT OF ST. MARK'S SUNDAY—SCHOOL,
>EASTER, 1881.

Copy of Certificate of First Incorporation of St. Mark's Church.

City and County of New York, ss :

Be it remembered that, in the year of our Lord one thousand and seven hundred and ninety-nine, on the eighteenth day of October, being the festival of St. Luke the Evangelist, at St. Mark's Church in the Bowery, immediately after divine service, a meeting of the male adult members of that congregation was held, in pursuance of notice to them given in time of morning service on the Twentieth and Twenty-first Sundays after Trinity, for the purpose of incorporating themselves under and conformable to the directions of the statute of this State entitled "An Act for the Relief of the Protestant Episcopal Church in the State of New York," at which time and place Peter Stuyvesant was called to the chair and Anthony Bleecker and Andrew Hamersley were chosen assistants, to preside at and conduct the proceedings of the meeting.

Who certify that by a majority of voices Peter Stuyvesant and Francis Bayard Winthrop were elected and chosen churchwardens, and Gilbert Colden Willett, Mangle Minthorne, Martin Hoffman, William Ogden, William A. Hardenbrook, George Turnbull, Nicholas William Stuyvesant and James Cummings were elected and chosen vestrymen.

And we also certify, that the said meeting did determine that Tuesday in Easter week the said offices of churchwardens and vestrymen should yearly forever thereafter cease, and their successors in office be elected and chosen.

And we do further certify that the said meeting did determine and resolve that the name, style and title by which the said church or congregation should be recognized by law, should be " The Rector, churchwardens and vestrymen of the Protestant Episcopal Church of St. Mark's in the Bowery, in the City of New York."

In witness whereof we have hereunto subscribed our names and affixed our seals, this eleventh day of October, in the year of our Lord one thousand seven hundred and ninety-nine.

      (Signed) Pr. Stuyvesant,
            A. L. Bleecker,
            Andrew Hamersly.

Signed and sealed in presence of
  Peter Gerard Stuyvesant,
  John Bleecker.

City of New York, ss.:

On the first day of November, in the year of our Lord one thousand seven hundred and ninety-nine, before me, Richard Harison, Esquire, recorder of the City of New York, personally appeared John Bleecker, who upon oath said that he was present and saw Peter Stuyvesant, Anthony L. Bleecker and Andrew Hamersley, within mentioned, sign and acknowledge the within written certificate, and that Peter Gerard Stuyvesant and himself did subscribe their names thereto as witnesses thereof, and I, having perused the same and finding therein no erasures or interlineations, do allow it to be recorded.

(Signed)   RICH. HARISON.

Recorded in the office of Clerk of the City and County of New York, in Lib. No. 1 of Religious Denominations, page 25, this 22nd day of November, 1799.

Examined by ROB. BENSON, Clk.

Opinion of Messrs. Troup, Hamilton and Harison

in the matter of a transfer of lots from Trinity to St. Mark's:

In consequence of a resolution of the Vestry of Trinity Church, of the ninth of November instant, we have considered the subject therein mentioned, and are of opinion that the Corporation of St. Mark's Church can have no valid pretensions, either at law or in equity, to any part of the property of the rector and inhabitants of the City of New York, in communion of the Protestant Episcopal Church, in the State of New York; but nevertheless, for greater caution, we approve of their taking from the Corporation of St. Mark's Church a deed in the form of that marked "A," when the lots lately set apart for that purpose are conveyed to the said Corporation.

New York, the 21st of November, 1801.

ROBT. TROUP,
ALEXANDER HAMILTON,
RICH. HARISON.

The deed so marked "A" was approved and executed, and is as follows:

To all to whom these Presents shall come or may in any wise concern: We, the rector, churchwardens and vestry of the Protestant Episcopal Church of St. Mark's in the Bowery, in the City of New York, send greeting; Whereas, the Corporation having the name and style of the rector and inhabitants of the City of New York, in communion of the Protestant Episcopal Church, in the State of New York, have, from their zeal to promote the cause of religion and piety, contributed largely to the expense of building St. Mark's Church aforesaid, and to the support of a clergyman to officiate and perform Divine Service therein, according to the rites and ceremonies of the said Protestant Episcopal Church, and have agreed to convey to us thirty lots of land, part of their real estate, for our own use and the purposes aforesaid; and, whereas, it may be deemed expedient by the said Corporation of the rector and inhabitants of the City of New York, in communion of the Protestant Episcopal Church, in the State of New York, to obviate and prevent any possibility of a question as to the residue of their real estate, or any claim or demand being ever made by us, or our successors, of, in or to the said estate, or any part, parcel, or member thereof, for or by reason of our belonging to the Protestant Episcopal Church ; Now, therefore, know ye, that we, the rector, churchwardens and vestry of St. Mark's Church in the Bowery, in consideration of the premises, and in order to prevent any doubt upon the question aforesaid, and to remove the possibility of any dispute or controversy that may in any manner disturb or interrupt the harmony, concord and affection which ought to prevail, and which we sincerely pray may prevail among the members of the said church, and also for and in consideration of one dollar to us in hand paid by the rector and inhabitants of the City of New York, in communion of the Protestant Episcopal Church, in the State of New York, the receipt whereof is hereby acknowledged, Do expressly, for us and our successors, disclaim and renounce all right, title, claim and demand whatsoever, of, in or to the real estate of the said rector and inhabitants of the City of New York, in communion of the Protestant Episcopal Church, of the State of New York, and of, in and to every or any part, share, property, or proportion thereof whatsoever, except what hath been voluntarily given and conveyed by them to us. And that all possibility of doubt upon the said subject may be removed, we do, for the consideration aforesaid, hereby clearly and absolutely renounce, release and grant unto the said Corporation having the name of the rector and inhabitants of the City of New York, in communion of the Protestant Episcopal Church, in the State of New York, all the right, title, interest, share, property, claim and demand whatsoever, both at law and in equity, which we now have, or which we, or our successors, may at any time or times hereafter have, challenge or claim, of, in and to the estate, lands and tenements belonging to the said rector and inhabitants of the City of New York, in communion of the Protestant Episcopal Church, in the State of New York, or possessed by them or their tenants, or any of them, so that neither we nor our successors shall ever hereafter have or claim any part of the said property, except such as we may have by the grant and conveyance of the said rector and inhabitants of the City of New York, in communion of the Protestant Episcopal Church, in the State of New York, as aforesaid.

In witness whereof, etc.

Deed for a Pew in St. Mark's Church.

This Indenture, made the   day of   , in the year of our Lord one thousand eight hundred and   **Between** the RECTOR, CHURCHWARDENS, AND VESTRY OF THE PROTESTANT EPISCOPAL CHURCH OF ST. MARK'S IN THE BOWERY, in the City of New York, of the first part, and
                         of the said City, of the second part, **Witnesseth**, That the parties of the first part, for and in consideration of the sum of   dollars, to them in hand paid by the said party of the second part, the receipt whereof is hereby acknowledged, have granted, and by these presents do grant, unto the said party of the second part, all that certain Pew in this Church, called St. Mark's, fronting on Stuyvesant Street, between the Second and Third Avenues, in the said City, said Pew being situate on the   of the said Church, and known as Pew number   **To Have and to Hold** the same, unto the said party of the second part,   heirs and assigns professing to belong to the Protestant Episcopal Church, so long as the said Church shall endure, subject to an annual rent of
        dollars, payable half yearly, on the first day of May and November, in each and every year forever.

Provided always, and these presents are upon this express condition, that if default shall at any time be made in the payment of said rent, or of any part thereof, for the space of one year after the same shall have become due as aforesaid, or if the said party of the second part,   heirs or assigns, shall at any time hereafter assign, transfer, or in any way make or set over the said Pew to any person or persons whatsoever, without the consent of the said parties of the first part, or their successors, under their seal, first had and obtained, or shall make any change or alteration in the said Pew, so as to alter the uniform appearance thereof, without the consent of the said parties of the first part, or their successors; then and from thenceforth these presents shall cease, and the grant hereby made shall be void, and it shall be lawful for the said parties of the first part, and their successors, to re-enter on the said Pew, and to have and hold and possess the same to their own use, or to sell or otherwise dispose of the said Pew, in like manner as though these presents had never been made.

In Witness Whereof, the said parties of the first part have caused their corporate seal to be hereto affixed, and the said party of the second part hath hereunto set   hand and seal the day and year first above written.

Letters Declining the Rectorship of St. Mark's Church in 1800 and 1801.

I. From the Rev. John Henry Hobart.

HEMPSTEAD, Septr. 18th, 1800.
Sir:
The proposals from Trinity church, which were in contemplation when you conversed with me, have now terminated in my connection with it as an assistant minister.

Tho' you are probably acquainted with this circumstance, yet I deem it respectful to inform you of it.

For the good intentions of the Vestry of St. Mark's Church towards me, I beg them to receive my grateful acknowledgments. In any other circumstances, the situation which they offered me would have appeared eligible and opened the prospect of usefulness. Tho' now precluded from the endeavour immediately to contribute thereto, yet no circumstance will give me greater pleasure than to hear of the prosperity and happiness of St. Mark's church.

I am, Sir, very respectfully,
Your obdt. Servt.,
J. H. HOBART.

Addressed:
William Ogden, Esq.,
Care of Mr. Peter Mackie,
67 Water Street,
New York.

II. From the Rev. Philander Chase.

POUGHKEEPSIE, Decemr. 20, 1800.
Respected Gentlemen:
This day, I have had the honour of receiving your letter to me, dated the 16th of the present month, with the resolution of the Vestry of St. Mark's Church accompanying the same.

According to your expressed request for a speedy answer, I immediately called a meeting of the vestry of the Church, to which I stood engaged, laid before them your proposals, and begged their opinion and determinations on the subject.

After canvassing the matter in question, they came to the resolution which I, herewith, send for your, and the vestry's, perusal.

I most sincerely wish that the Vestry of St. Mark's will put the most favourable construction on what has been done; as I am fully of opinion that the vestry of the Church in this place has acted on laudable principles, what they candidly thought was for the best, both for my own interest, and that of the Church in general.

The Vestry of St. Mark's will be pleased to accept my best wishes for their prosperity, and believe me to be their
Most obedient
humble servant,
PHILANDER CHASE.

Messrs.
Prs. Stuyvesant
and
George Turnbull.
Addressed:
Prs. Stuyvesant, Esqr.,
Bowery-house,
New York.

Extract from minutes of Vestry of Christ Church, Poughkeepsie:

POUGHKEEPSIE, Decemr. 20th, 1800.

At a Meeting of the Vestry of Christ's Church of this Place on Saturday, the 20th Decr., 1800.
Present:
The Revd. Philander Chase, Rector.
John Reade, Church Warden.

John Mott,
John P. Vemont,   } Vestrymen. { William Davis,
Archd. Stewart,   Ebenezer Badger,
Robert Noxon,   Stephen Hoyt.

A Letter was laid before the Vestry by the Revd. Mr. Chase from a Committee of the Vestry of St. Mark's Church, New York, giving him a Call to the Rectorship of that Church; with a Salary of One Thousand Dollars ye Year.

On which the Vestry on Mature deliberation are of opinion, that the proposed Salary of One Thousand Dollars wou'd not Materially advance the Pecuniary Advantage of Mr. Chase, that his removal from the Parish of Poughkeepsie at this time wou'd essentially injure the progress and Growth of our Church, as no one of the Congregation, but holds the Revd. Mr. Chase in the highest estimation; and that his removal at this time wou'd be destructive of the Interest of the Episcopal Church in this Place and in effect destroy its present Flourishing State.

Therefore Resolved that the Vestry, upon the foregoing reasons, cannot think of discharging the Rev. Mr. Chase from his engagements with this Congregation on the terms offered in the Resolution of the Vestry of St. Mark's Church in New York.

Dated 12th December, 1800.

Extract from the Minutes of Vestry.
By Order of Vestry,
STEPHEN HOYT, Clrk.

III. FROM THE REV. CAVE JONES.

ACCOMACK, 26 Jany., 1801.

FRANCIS B. WINTHROP, } Esqs.
WILLIAM OGDEN,

Gentlemen:

As my answer returned to your favour was rather indeterminate, I take the liberty, lest you should remain in uncertainty, of informing you, that just about the same time of that's coming to

hand I rec'd from the Vestry of Trinity Church an Invitation to that living, of which I have seen proper to accept. It gives me pleasure that my situation is likely to be established so near to St. Mark's, that so, altho' not their stated Pastor, I may at least have an opportunity of joining with them in occasional service.
With sentiments of perfect respect to the
members of the Vestry of St. Mark's generally,
I am, Gentlemen,
Your Obedt. Servt.,
Addressed: CAVE JONES.
Francis Bayd. Winthrop, Esq.,
New York.

IV. FROM THE REV. THEODORE DEHON.

TO THE VESTRY OF ST. MARK'S CHURCH, NEAR NEW YORK.

Gentlemen:
Your resolve of the 16th ulto., inviting me to the rectorship of your Church, was politely communicated to me by the Committee nominated by you for the purpose.
The prospect which your Church presents is indeed an inviting one. My temporal interests would be greatly promoted by an acceptance of your call, and I could look forward to the enjoyment of much spiritual and social satisfaction in connection with a society for which I have already entertained warm sentiments of esteem. But after considering the subject in every view, in which your benefit and my duty appear'd to be involved, I feel myself obliged, not without some reluctance, to decline accepting your invitation. The people of my present cure have so bound my affections to them by their endearing attention to my ministry, and discover such painful concern at the suggestion of my removal, that to separate from them would require a struggle which I know not how to sustain. Nothing in the present circumstances of my connection with them would reconcile me to it but the unfavourableness of this situation to my health, and this, perhaps, ought not to influence me till by a longer residence I shall have made a more conclusive experiment.
I pray you, Gentlemen, to be assured of my deep sense of the honour conferred on me by your resolve, of my devout prayers that the supreme head of the Church would furnish you with a rector in every respect more able and worthy, than myself, to build you up in his most holy faith.
THEODORE DEHON.
NEWPORT, Nov. 9th, 1801.

The Annual Memorial Service at St. Mark's Church on All Saints' Day.

A glance at the names in this book will show how intimately St. Mark's is connected with the history of the city in its three stages, Dutch, English and American. It stands on the oldest continuous church site on Manhattan Island. A Dutch, an English and an American Governor lie buried in its precincts. Its parishioners have been members of the city, state and national governments, and of the colonial governments as well. Scattered through the various parishes of the city are to be found many descendants of families who once gathered within its walls. Its vaults are still being frequently opened to receive their dead.

Thus St. Mark's occupies a peculiar position among the churches. Whatever changes have taken place in the *personnel* of its worshippers, whatever part it may be called upon to play in its next century in ministering to the spiritual needs of a different population from that of the last, in one respect at least there will be no change: It will always be a centre of interest to a large number of persons, because their ancestors lie buried in its oil and the traditions of their families are so closely interwoven with the traditions of the Church.

St. Mark's, on its part, gladly recognizes the tie which binds it to the children of its early parishioners, and it will always delight to have them look upon it as the old spiritual home. Such historic associations cannot easily be broken. St. Mark's has no wish to weaken the ties which bind those descendants to other parishes; but it must hope that occasionally they will come back to the old mother church. And it feels that at some time in each year there should be a service especially for their sake.

The present rector, in the beginning of his incumbency, held a memorial service on All Saints' Day, November 1st, 1899, with the above object in view, and expressed his desire that that service should become an annual institution.

Fully conscious of the need of devoting its energies to the spiritual welfare of the people, who have come to dwell in its neighborhood, St. Mark's itself does not wish to forget the past, and it hopes that those, who are linked to its history by family traditions, will on All Saints' Day remember the place where their ancestors were wont to worship God.

www.ingramcontent.com/pod-product-compliance
Lightning Source LLC
Chambersburg PA
CBHW022018220426
43663CB00007B/1127